MARK HADDON is the author of three novels, including *The Curious Incident of the Dog in the Night-Time* and *The Red House*, and a volume of poetry, *The Talking Horse and the Sad Girl and the Village Under the Sea*. He has written drama for stage, TV and radio. His latest book, a collection of short stories, is *The Pier Falls*, published by Jonathan Cape.

STATES OF MIND: *Tracing the Edges of Consciousness* is an exhibition developed by Wellcome Collection to interrogate our understanding of the conscious experience. Exploring phenomena such as somnambulism, synaesthesia and disorders of memory, the exhibition examines ideas around the nature of consciousness, and in particular what can happen when our typical conscious experience is interrupted, damaged or undermined.

WELLCOME COLLECTION is the free visitor destination for the incurably curious. It explores the connections between medicine, life and art in the past, present and future. Wellcome Collection is part of the Wellcome Trust, a global charitable foundation dedicated to improving health by supporting bright minds in science, the humanities and social sciences, and public engagement.

A collection of literature, science, philosophy and art

STATES OF MIND

Experiences at the Edge of Consciousness

Introduction by Mark Haddon

Edited by Anna Faherty

First published in the United Kingdom in 2016
by Wellcome Collection, part of The Wellcome Trust
215 Euston Road
London NW1 2BE.

Published for the Wellcome Collection exhibition
States of Mind: Tracing the Edges of Consciousness,
curated by Emily Sargent.

wellcome collection

www.wellcomecollection.org

Wellcome Collection is part of the Wellcome Trust,
a global charitable foundation dedicated to achieving
extraordinary improvements in human and animal
health.

A CIP catalogue record for this book is available
from the British Library.

ISBN 978-1-78125-655-8

Editor: Anna Faherty
Editorial: Rob Reddick
Design: Studio Hato
Printed in Great Britain by Clays Ltd

Any omissions and errors of attribution are uninten-
tional and will, if notified in writing to the editor, care of
the Wellcome Trust, be corrected in future printings.

Contents

2: Sleep | Awake

3: Language | Memory

4: Being | Not Being

The Hardest Problem
Mark Haddon

My son's nine-year-old friend Yahya said it most succinctly. *Why is life in the first person?*

We think. We feel. We are aware of ourselves and the world around us. We have consciousness. We are made of the same raw materials as bacteria, as earth, as rock, as the great dark nebulae of dust that swim between the stars, as the stars themselves. But somehow, a vanishingly small fraction of that brute stuff (you, me, chimpanzees maybe, chickens possibly, worms probably not) has been cunningly arranged into objects which experience what William James calls "subjective life" (p. 51). How is that possible? Why do most of us feel that we are something more than molecules? Why are even ardent materialists haunted by the sense of being something insubstantial inhabiting a physical vessel?

The writings in this book go back only 500 years, but the ancient Egyptians already had a sophisticated model of a five-part soul attached to an earthly body. Doubtless simpler models go back much, much further. It is a puzzle which, in its manifold cognate forms, has fascinated, divided and defined human culture for at least as long as we have been able to write about these things. What do we mean by the soul? Does it live on after death? Can we be reincarnated in the body of someone not yet born? When does consciousness begin and when does it end? Do dreams give us access to some deeper truth? Can evil spirits possess us? What happens on that strange borderland between the conscious and the unconscious? Can we be held responsible for what we do while we are asleep? Can multiple personalities really share one body? Do you see red in the same way that I see red? Are animals conscious? Could a computer think and feel and be aware?

When I was nine years old I was obsessed by a question

similar to Yahya's. *Why am I me?* It seemed extraordinary
that of all possible times and places I was born in England in
1962. It gave me a thrilling shiver to think that I had narrowly
escaped one of the terrifying lives I knew children lived in
other centuries and in other parts of the world.

I knew, even then, that there was something wrong with
the question. It wasn't possible for me to be anyone else. I
was this body. I wasn't a blob of spiritual jam which had been
squirted into a material doughnut when I entered the world.
It was this life which had made me. But that knowledge didn't
drive out the conviction that I was on the *inside* looking *out*.
Turning this paradox over and over in my mind I felt as if I'd
stumbled on a missed stitch in the fabric of the universe and
that if I tugged and worried at it for long enough I might be
able to tease out a loose strand and discover what the world
was made of.

Two other subjects obsessed me as a boy, as they obsessed
many people in the early 1970s: cosmology and particle
physics. I'd stayed up for the moon landing in July 1969. I
watched documentaries about relativity and black holes. We
did Young's double-slit experiment at school to show that light
was a wave despite also being a particle. I was certain that
the world was on the brink of an Answer to Everything, and
I'm sure I wasn't alone in thinking that. But with every new
development, every new discovery (cosmic inflation, string
theory, the top quark, the Bose–Einstein condensate...) the
explanations felt less like explanations and more like complica-
tions. Increasingly the physics of the very big and the physics
of the very small were becoming a matter of finding the maths
to fit the data. As Richard Feynman said of quantum theory, "If
you think you understand... then you don't." It's hard to read
about the multiverse, for example, or look at a map of micro-
wave background radiation from the early universe and sense
the jigsaw falling into place, as you might when reading for the

first time about Darwin's theory of evolution or the heliocentrism of Copernican or Newtonian mechanics.

I can still think about the puzzle of consciousness, however, and feel the same infuriating, obsessive fascination I felt as a child.

Over the last 50 years biology, neuroscience and psychology have made huge advances in solving what David Chalmers called the "easy" problems of consciousness[1], the questions of how the brain performs (and sometimes fails to perform) its mechanical and computational functions: how we remember, how we process information from the external world, how we direct our attention, how we make judgements and take decisions... But we are no nearer to solving what he called the "hard" problem, the question of why we experience these things from the inside, as subjects.

The problem still nags at me. How difficult can it be? The raw material is not squirreled away inside an atom. It didn't happen 14 billion years ago. It's not hiding on the other side of the universe. It's right here. Stop reading and look around the room, become aware of your feet, remember what you were doing yesterday. How is it possible for a lump of oxygen, carbon, hydrogen, nitrogen, calcium and potassium to do these things? I can't shake the conviction that some kind of answer is just around the corner but I still have absolutely no idea what kind of answer it might be.

Indeed, far from solving the puzzle, recent advances in biology, neuroscience and psychology have, if anything, made it more complex. It is getting more and more difficult to fall back on the idea that there is some kind of ghost in the machine[2], the idea, most famously posited by Descartes, that the mind is a non-material entity connected to a material body. We understand the working of the brain in rapidly increasing detail and while what Edgar Allan Poe called "the magic pinions and the wizard wheels" (p. 217) are breathtakingly complex, it really does look like it's just molecules in there. No one has yet stumbled on what Francis Galton called the "presence-chamber" of the mind (p. 30). Everything so far observed inside the human head is a chemical reaction, an event which happens automatically when the right molecules are in the right place in the right state at the right time.

Materialism – the belief that everything in the universe is made exclusively of matter and that all mental events are therefore identical to interactions between matter – seems to be winning. Indeed there are many philosophers and scientists who believe that it has already won. But it feels like a pyrrhic victory. We are getting closer and closer to knowing precisely what happens in the brain when we juggle, or taste lasagne, or recognise an angry face, but this offers us no help in explaining how and why those things are *experiences*, only in showing the neural correlate, the stuff that happens in the brain at the same time. It may very well be that there is no ghost in the machine, but how on earth does a machine give itself the impression that there is one?

The puzzle has, to a large extent, been monopolised in recent years by philosophy and neuroscience, and it has become generally accepted that the languages of philosophy and neuroscience are the correct ones to use when discussing the subject. As a result much writing about consciousness is complex at best and impenetrable at worst, and experts in neighbouring fields who are understandably tempted to stray into the area risk sounding naive and ill-informed.

This book ignores that monopoly. It admits that there are many languages in which we can explore the subject of consciousness. It celebrates ambiguity and contradiction, ignorance and simplicity. It makes no assumptions and feels free to ask any question, however obscure and eccentric it might seem.

The subject is vast and approaching it in this manner

makes it exponentially larger. So this book focuses on disrupted and liminal states of consciousness, what happens when consciousness fails or falters, what happens at the outer limits of consciousness – out-of-body experiences and teleportation, multiple personality, sleep and dreams, the slips of language and memory, anaesthesia and death.

It takes evidence from people who have remained awake during operations. It hears from hypnotists. It contains the words of poets and artists, the dreaming and the dying. It suggests that writers of fiction, who spend their days arranging words to make readers forget themselves and enter, for a brief time, into the consciousness of characters who don't exist, might have something important to contribute. Because, if nothing else, the passages printed here should convince you that novelists, poets and artists have intuitively understood many of the mind's oddities since long before doctors and scientists began taking an interest. Hopefully it should persuade readers to treat all writing about consciousness with sceptical fascination and encourage them to ask their own questions and come to their own conclusions.

If there were more pages we might consider the minds of chimpanzees and octopi and hear what Buddhism has to say about everyday consciousness. We might see the visions of Hildegard of Bingen and visit John Searle's Chinese room. We might encounter Phineas Gage and philosophical zombies.

One of the areas the book hasn't had the space to cover in depth is the experience of those people who are labelled as having learning difficulties and psychiatric illnesses, a subject which highlights an important issue.

We don't talk about consciousness in the way that we talk about other mental faculties. We are happy to say that one person has a very good memory, that a second person takes little notice of their surroundings, or that a third has a wonderful imagination. We accept that some people are unable to see or hear as clearly as other people. But we look upon consciousness as something of a different order, the greater frame within which all these lesser faculties are set, the mental theatre in which the drama of the world seems to be played out for us, something singular and monolithic gifted equally to all human beings. You either have it or you don't.

This way of thinking is due, in part, to the relationship between the idea of consciousness and the idea of the soul, so that the former retains some of the sacred glow which was previously attached to the latter. Consequently to say that your consciousness differs from mine feels tantamount to saying that one of us is more human than the other.

Except that consciousness is neither singular nor monolithic. As many passages in the book make clear, the frame within which some people's faculties are set is radically different from that of others. And those individual frames can change radically over the years, as a result of accident and disease, of growth and ageing.

You might have a short-term memory less than a minute long and yet be wholly unaware of this fact. You might experience the universe as empty and meaningless. You might experience the universe as a firework display of stimuli, significance, opportunity and temptation. You might swing unpredictably between these two states. You might be unable to conceive that other people are conscious in the way that you are conscious, and therefore have difficulty interacting with them. You might be unable to focus on the present moment because you are haunted by the past and frightened by the future. You might hear inanimate objects talking. You might hear voices inside your own head. You might find abstract thought well-nigh impossible.

We fall too easily into the trap of thinking that, on the one hand, there is the healthy, functioning consciousness of 'normal' people, and on the other hand there is the unhealthy, damaged consciousness of 'abnormal' people, people we class as ill or damaged or mentally diminished in some way. But that says more about society than about consciousness itself. In truth no way of experiencing the world is intrinsically more or less valid than any other. And all of them are fascinating and informative.

Why is life in the first person?

We may never find a truly satisfying and conclusive answer. We may realise that it was the wrong question altogether. But you will never really know what it is like to be me and I will never really know what it is like to be you. And this very unknowability of other human beings is, in large part, what fuels our fascination with poetry and fiction and art, those windows into other minds. And as for the puzzle of why it is *like anything* to be either you or me, that promises to remain one of the deep and abiding mysteries of the universe for a long time.

1 Chalmers DJ. Facing up to the problem of consciousness. J Conscious Stud 1995;2(3):200–19.
2 The phrase was coined by Gilbert Ryle in his 1949 book *The Concept of Mind*.

1: Science | Soul

Body and soul | *Life and death* |
Dissociation | *Spirit world* | Inner
struggle | *Heart and mind* | Location
of the soul | *Nature of body and soul* |
Consciousness of others | *Awareness
of self* | Visions | *Second sight* |
Brain structure | *Thought processes* |
Meditation | *The self* | Identity | *Artificial
consciousness* | Projecting consciousness
| *Machine thinking* | Conscious thought |
Neuroscience | Studying consciousness
| *The nervous system* | Synaesthesia |
Touching the soul | Sense perception
| *Multiple personalities* | Hypnosis |
The subconscious

'Body and Soul Must Part'
Robert Blair, 1743

In this extract from 'The Grave' Scottish poet and clergyman Robert Blair (1699–1746) describes the pain of the "frantick soul" as it separates from its now redundant body.

How shocking must thy Summons be, O *Death*!
To him that is at Ease in his Possessions;
Who counting on long Years of Pleasure here,
Is quite unfurnish'd for that World to come!
In that dread Moment, how the frantick Soul
Raves round the Walls of her Clay Tenement,
Runs to each Avenue, and shrieks for Help,
But shrieks in vain! How wishfully she looks
On all she's leaving, now no longer hers!
A little longer, yet a little longer,
Oh! Might she stay, to wash away her Stains,
And fit her for her Passage! Mournful Sight!
Her very Eyes weep Blood; and every Groan
She heaves is big with Horror: But the Foe,
Like a stanch Murth'rer steady to his Purpose,
Pursues her close through ev'ry Lane of Life,
Nor misses once the Track, but presses on;
Till forc'd at last to the tremendous Verge,
At once she sinks to everlasting Ruin.

Sure! 'tis a serious Thing to *Die*! My Soul!
What a strange moment must it be, when near
The Journey's End, thou hast the Gulf in View?
That awful Gulf no Mortal e're repass'd
To tell what's doing on the other Side!

Nature runs back, and shudders at the Sight,
And every Life-string bleeds at Thoughts of parting!
For part they must: *Body* and *Soul* must part;
Fond Couple! link'd more close than wedded Pair.
This wings its Way to its Almighty Source,
The Witness of its Actions, now its Judge:
That drops into the dark and noisome *Grave*,
Like a disabled Pitcher of no Use.

The Soul Hovering over the Body Reluctantly Parting with Life
Luigi Schiavonetti after William Blake, 1808

The distinction between the inanimate body and conscious soul is starkly apparent in this illustration of the final moments of life, commissioned to accompany Robert Blair's poem 'The Grave'.

The Soul hovering over the Body reluctantly parting with Life.

The Stolen Body
H G Wells, 1898

> When liberal-minded lawyer Mr Bessel dissociates his
> mind from his physical form in H G Wells's (1866–1946)
> short story *The Stolen Body*, disastrous consequences
> ensue. In this extract, Bessel's experiences in a "state
> outside this world" are reported. The narrator postulates
> that the bodiless beings Bessel encounters may be men
> lost in madness.

The release was, [Bessel] asserts, instantaneous. "At one
moment I was seated in my chair, with my eyes tightly shut,
my hands gripping the arms of the chair, doing all I could to
concentrate my mind on Vincent, and then I perceived myself
outside my body – saw my body near me, but certainly not
containing me, with the hands relaxing and the head drooping
forward on the breast."

Nothing shakes him in his assurance of that release. He
describes in a quiet, matter-of-fact way the new sensation he
experienced. He felt he had become impalpable – so much
he had expected, but he had not expected to find himself
enormously large. So, however, it would seem he became.
"I was a great cloud – if I may express it that way – anchored
to my body. It appeared to me, at first, as if I had discovered a
greater self of which the conscious being in my brain was only
a little part. I saw the Albany and Piccadilly and Regent Street
and all the rooms and places in the houses, very minute and
very bright and distinct, spread out below me like a little city
seen from a balloon. Every now and then vague shapes like
drifting wreaths of smoke made the vision a little indistinct,
but at first I paid little heed to them. The thing that astonished
me most, and which astonishes me still, is that I saw quite
distinctly the insides of the houses as well as the streets, saw

little people dining and talking in the private houses, men and women dining, playing billiards, and drinking in restaurants and hotels, and several places of entertainment crammed with people. It was like watching the affairs of a glass hive."

Such were Mr Bessel's exact words as I took them down when he told me the story. Quite forgetful of Mr Vincent, he remained for a space observing these things. Impelled by curiosity, he says, he stooped down, and with the shadowy arm he found himself possessed of attempted to touch a man walking along Vigo Street. But he could not do so, though his finger seemed to pass through the man. Something prevented his doing this, but what it was he finds it hard to describe. He compares the obstacle to a sheet of glass.

"I felt as a kitten may feel," he said, "when it goes for the first time to pat its reflection in a mirror." Again and again, on the occasion when I heard him tell this story, Mr Bessel returned to that comparison of the sheet of glass. Yet it was not altogether a precise comparison, because, as the reader will speedily see, there were interruptions of this generally impermeable resistance, means of getting through the barrier to the material world again. But, naturally, there is a very great difficulty in expressing these unprecedented impressions in the language of everyday experience.

A thing that impressed him instantly, and which weighed upon him throughout all this experience, was the stillness of this place – he was in a world without sound.

At first Mr Bessel's mental state was an unemotional wonder. His thought chiefly concerned itself with where he might be. He was out of the body – out of his material body, at any rate – but that was not all. He believes, and I for one believe also, that he was somewhere out of space, as we understand it, altogether. By a strenuous effort of will he had passed out of his body into a world beyond this world, a world undreamt of, yet lying so close to it and so strangely situated with regard to it that all things on this earth are clearly visible both from without and from within in this other world about us. For a long time, as it seemed to him, this realisation occupied his mind to the exclusion of all other matters, and then he recalled the engagement with Mr Vincent, to which this astonishing experience was, after all, but a prelude.

He turned his mind to locomotion in this new body in which he found himself. For a time he was unable to shift himself from his attachment to his earthly carcass. For a time this new strange cloud body of his simply swayed, contracted, expanded, coiled, and writhed with his efforts to free himself, and then quite suddenly the link that bound him snapped. For a moment everything was hidden by what appeared to be whirling spheres of dark vapour, and then through a moment-ary gap he saw his drooping body collapse limply, saw his lifeless head drop sideways, and found he was driving along like a huge cloud in a strange place of shadowy clouds that had the luminous intricacy of London spread like a model below.

But now he was aware that the fluctuating vapour about him was something more than vapour, and the temerarious excitement of his first essay was shot with fear. For he perceived, at first indistinctly, and then suddenly very clearly, that he was surrounded by *faces!* That each roll and coil of the seeming cloud-stuff was a face. And such faces! Faces of thin shadow, faces of gaseous tenuity. Faces like those faces that glare with intolerable strangeness upon the sleeper in the evil hours of his dreams. Evil, greedy eyes that were full of a covetous curiosity, faces with knit brows and snarling, smiling lips; their vague hands clutched at Mr Bessel as he passed, and the rest of their bodies was but an elusive streak of trailing darkness. Never a word they said, never a sound from the mouths that seemed to gibber. All about him they pressed in that dreamy silence, passing freely through the dim mistiness that was his body, gathering ever more numerously about him. And the shadowy Mr Bessel, now suddenly fear-stricken, drove through the silent, active multitude of eyes and clutching hands.

So inhuman were these faces, so malignant their staring eyes, and shadowy, clawing gestures, that it did not occur to Mr Bessel to attempt intercourse with these drifting creatures. Idiot phantoms, they seemed, children of vain desire, beings unborn and forbidden the boon of being, whose only expressions and gestures told of the envy and craving for life that was their one link with existence.

It says much for his resolution that, amidst the swarming cloud of these noiseless spirits of evil, he could still think of Mr Vincent. He made a violent effort of will and found himself, he knew not how, stooping towards Staple Inn, saw Vincent sitting attentive and alert in his arm-chair by the fire.

And clustering also about him, as they clustered ever about all that lives and breathes, was another multitude of these vain, voiceless shadows, longing, desiring, seeking some loophole into life.

For a space Mr Bessel sought ineffectually to attract his friend's attention. He tried to get in front of his eyes, to move the objects in his room, to touch him. But Mr Vincent remained unaffected, ignorant of the being that was so close to his own. The strange something that Mr Bessel has compared to a sheet of glass separated them impermeably.

And at last Mr Bessel did a desperate thing. I have told how that in some strange way he could see not only the outside of a man as we see him, but within. He extended his shadowy hand and thrust his vague black fingers, as it seemed, through the heedless brain.

Then, suddenly, Mr Vincent started like a man who recalls his attention from wandering thoughts, and it seemed to Mr Bessel that a little dark-red body situated in the middle of Mr Vincent's brain swelled and glowed as he did so. Since that experience he has been shown anatomical figures of the brain, and he knows now that this is that useless structure, as doctors call it, the pineal eye. For, strange as it will seem to many, we have, deep in our brains – where it cannot possibly see any earthly light – an eye! At the time this, with the rest of the internal anatomy of the brain, was quite new to him. At the sight of its changed appearance, however, he thrust forth his finger, and, rather fearful still of the consequences, touched this little spot. And instantly Mr Vincent started, and Mr Bessel knew that he was seen.

And at that instant it came to Mr Bessel that evil had happened to his body, and behold! a great wind blew through all that world of shadows and tore him away. So strong was this persuasion, that he thought no more of Mr Vincent, but turned about forthwith, and all the countless faces drove back with him like leaves before a gale. But he returned too late. In an instant he saw the body that he had left inert and collapsed – lying, indeed, like the body of a man just dead – had arisen, had arisen by virtue of some strength and will beyond his own. It stood with staring eyes, stretching its limbs in dubious fashion.

For a moment he watched it in wild dismay, and then he stooped towards it. But the pane of glass had closed against him again, and he was foiled. He beat himself passionately against this, and all about him the spirits of evil grinned and pointed and mocked. He gave way to furious anger. He compares himself to a bird that has fluttered heedlessly into a room and is beating at the window-pane that holds it back from freedom.

And behold! the little body that had once been his was now dancing with delight. He saw it shouting, though he could not hear its shouts; he saw the violence of its movements grow. He watched it fling his cherished furniture about in the mad delight of existence, rend his books apart, smash bottles, drink heedlessly from the jagged fragments, leap and smite in a passionate acceptance of living. He watched these actions in paralysed astonishment. Then once more he hurled himself against the impassable barrier, and then, with all that crew of mocking ghosts about him, hurried back in dire confusion to Vincent to tell him of the outrage that had come upon him.

But the brain of Vincent was now closed against apparitions, and the disembodied Mr Bessel pursued him in vain as he hurried out into Holborn to call a cab. Foiled and terror-stricken, Mr Bessel swept back again, to find his desecrated body whooping in a glorious frenzy down the Burlington Arcade...

And now the attentive reader begins to understand Mr Bessel's interpretation of the first part of this strange story. The being whose frantic rush through London had inflicted so much injury and disaster had indeed Mr Bessel's body, but it was not Mr Bessel. It was an evil spirit out of that strange world beyond existence, into which Mr Bessel had so rashly ventured. For twenty hours it held possession of him, and for all those twenty hours the dispossessed spirit-body of Mr Bessel was going to and fro in that unheard-of middle world of shadows seeking help in vain.

He spent many hours beating at the minds of Mr Vincent and of his friend Mr Hart. Each, as we know, he roused by his efforts. But the language that might convey his situation to these helpers across the gulf he did not know; his feeble fingers groped vainly and powerlessly in their brains. Once, indeed, as we have already told, he was able to turn Mr Vincent aside from his path so that he encountered the stolen body in its career, but he could not make him understand the thing that had happened: he was unable to draw any help from that encounter...

All through those hours the persuasion was overwhelming in Mr Bessel's mind that presently his body would be killed by its furious tenant, and he would have to remain in this shadow-land for evermore. So that those long hours were a growing agony of fear. And ever as he hurried to and fro in his ineffectual excitement innumerable spirits of that world about him mobbed him and confused his mind. And ever an envious applauding multitude poured after their successful fellow as he went upon his glorious career.

For that, it would seem, must be the life of these bodiless things of this world that is the shadow of our world. Ever they watch, coveting a way into a mortal body, in order that they may descend, as furies and frenzies, as violent lusts and mad, strange impulses, rejoicing in the body they have won. For Mr Bessel was not the only human soul in that place. Witness the fact that he met first one, and afterwards several shadows of men, men like himself, it seemed, who had lost their bodies even it may be as he had lost his, and wandered, despairingly, in that lost world that is neither life nor death. They could not speak because that world is silent, yet he knew them for men because of their dim human bodies, and because of the sadness of their faces.

But how they had come into that world he could not tell, nor where the bodies they had lost might be, whether they still raved about the earth, or whether they were closed forever in death against return. That they were the spirits of the dead neither he nor I believe. But Doctor Wilson Paget thinks they are the rational souls of men who are lost in madness on the earth.

A Dialogue between the Soul and the Body
Andrew Marvell, 1681

English politician and poet Andrew Marvell (1621–1678)
depicts the internal war between an individual's body and
soul as a battle in which the final sally is made by the body.

Soul

O, Who shall, from this dungeon, raise
A soul enslaved so many ways?
With bolts of bones, that fettered stands
In feet, and manacled in hands;
Here blinded with an eye, and there
Deaf with the drumming of an ear;
A soul hung up, as 'twere, in chains
Of nerves, and arteries, and veins;
Tortured, besides each other part,
In a vain head, and double heart?

Body

O, who shall me deliver whole
From bonds of this tyrannic soul?
Which, stretched upright, impales me so
That mine own precipice I go;
And warms and moves this needless frame,
(A fever could but do the same,)
And, wanting where its spite to try,
Has made me live to let me die
A body that could never rest
Since this ill spirit it possessed.

Soul

What magic could me thus confine
Within another's grief to pine?
Where, whatsoever it complain,
I feel, that cannot feel, the pain;
And all my care itself employs,
That to preserve, which me destroys;
Constrained not only to endure
Diseases, but, what's worse, the cure;
And ready oft the port to gain,
Am shipwrecked into health again.

Body

But Physic yet could never reach
The maladies thou me dost teach;
Whom first the cramp of hope does tear,
And then the palsy shakes of fear;
The pestilence of love does heat,
Or hatred's hidden ulcer eat;
Joy's cheerful madness does perplex,
Or Sorrow's other madness vex;
Which knowledge forces me to know,
And memory will not foregoe;
What but a soul could have the wit
To build me up for sin so fit?
So architects do square and hew
Green trees that in the forest grew.

The Tin Woodman and the Scarecrow
W W Denslow, 1900

The Tin Woodman in American author L Frank Baum's
(1856–1919) fantasy novel *The Wonderful Wizard of Oz*
believes a heart, not a brain, makes one happy. The
Scarecrow chooses brains over a heart, leaving Dorothy
puzzled about which of her friends is right.

'Where the Soul Exercises Its Functions'
René Descartes, 1649

In his last published work, *The Passions of the Soul*,
French mathematician and philosopher René Descartes
(1596–1650) considers the physical location of the soul
and its actions.

Article XXX
That the soul is united to all the portions of the body conjointly.
But in order to understand all these things more perfectly, we
must know that the soul is really joined to the whole body, and
that we cannot, properly speaking, say that it exists in any one
of its parts to the exclusion of the others, because it is one and
in some manner indivisible, owing to the disposition of its
organs, which are so related to one another that when any one
of them is removed, that renders the whole body defective; and
because it is of a nature which has no relation to extension,
nor dimensions, nor other properties of the matter of which
the body is composed, but only to the whole conglomerate of
its organs, as appears from the fact that we could not in any
way conceive of the half or the third of a soul, nor of the space
it occupies, and because it does not become smaller owing to
the cutting off of some portion of the body, but separates itself
from it entirely when the union of its assembled organs is
dissolved.

Article XXXI
*That there is a small gland in the brain in which the soul exercises
its functions more particularly than in the other parts.*
It is likewise necessary to know that although the soul is joined
to the whole body, there is yet in that a certain part in which it
exercises its functions more particularly than in all the others;
and it is usually believed that this part is the brain, or possibly

the heart: the brain, because it is with it that the organs of
sense are connected, and the heart because it is apparently in it
that we experience the passions. But, in examining the matter
with care, it seems as though I had clearly ascertained that
the part of the body in which the soul exercises its functions
immediately is in nowise the heart, nor the whole of the brain,
but merely the most inward of all its parts, to wit, a certain very
small gland which is situated in the middle of its substance
and so suspended above the duct whereby the animal spirits
in its anterior cavities have communication with those in the
posterior, that the slightest movements which take place in it
may alter very greatly the course of these spirits; and recipro-
cally that the smallest changes which occur in the course of the
spirits may do much to change the movements of this gland.

'A Finely Fram'd and Well-Tun'd Organ-Case'
George Cheyne, 1733

> Scottish physician George Cheyne (*c*.1671–1743) wrote
> medical treatises for a popular audience. *The English Malady*
> shared his then-modernist views, depicting the body and
> soul as a lubricated machine.

These need only suppose, that the Human Body is a Machin
of an infinite Number and Variety of different Channels
and Pipes, filled with various and different Liquors and
Fluids, perpetually running, glideing, or creeping forward,
or returning backward, in a constant *Circle*, and sending out
little Branches and Outlets, to moisten, nourish, and repair
the Expences of Living. That the Intelligent Principle, or *Soul*,
resides somewhere in the Brain, where all the Nerves, or
Instruments of Sensation terminate, like a *Musician* in a finely
fram'd and well-tun'd Organ-Case; that these Nerves are like

Keys, which, being struck on or touch'd, convey the Sound and Harmony to this sentient Principle, or *Musician*.

Or, in a more gross Similitude, the Intelligen[t] Principle is like a Bell in a Steeple, to which there are an infinite Number of Hammers all around it, with Ropes of all Lengths, terminating or touching at every Point of the Surface of the Trunk or Case, one of whose Extremities being pull'd or touch'd by any *Body* whatsoever, conveys a measur'd, and proportion'd Impulse or Stroke to the Bell, which gives the proper Sound. These, or such like Similitudes, tho' Lame and Imperfect, are all, I doubt, was ever design'd for the Generality of Mankind in the Knowledge necessary towards *Health* and *Life*, in such Matters.

What Is It Like to Be a Bat?
Thomas Nagel, 1974

American philosopher Thomas Nagel (b. 1937) questioned the experience of bats to demonstrate that we can never truly understand what it is like to be someone else.

I assume we all believe that bats have experience. After all, they are mammals, and there is no more doubt that they have experience than that mice or pigeons or whales have experience. I have chosen bats instead of wasps or flounders because if one travels too far down the phylogenetic tree, people gradually shed their faith that there is experience there at all. Bats, although more closely related to us than those other species, nevertheless present a range of activity and a sensory apparatus so different from ours that the problem I want to pose is exceptionally vivid (though it certainly could be raised with other species). Even without the benefit of philosophical reflection, anyone who has spent some time in an enclosed

CONSCIOUSNESS OF OTHERS | PHILOSOPHY

space with an excited bat knows what it is to encounter a fundamentally *alien* form of life.

I have said that the essence of the belief that bats have experience is that there is something that it is like to be a bat. Now we know that most bats (the microchiroptera, to be precise) perceive the external world primarily by sonar, or echolocation, detecting the reflections, from objects within range, of their own rapid, subtly modulated, high-frequency shrieks. Their brains are designed to correlate the outgoing impulses with the subsequent echoes, and the information thus acquired enables bats to make precise discriminations of distance, size, shape, motion, and texture comparable to those we make by vision. But bat sonar, though clearly a form of perception, is not similar in its operation to any sense that we possess, and there is no reason to suppose that it is subjectively like anything we can experience or imagine. This appears to create difficulties for the notion of what it is like to be a bat. We must consider whether any method will permit us to extrapolate to the inner life of the bat from our own case[1], and if not, what alternative methods there may be for under-standing the notion.

Our own experience provides the basic material for our imagination, whose range is therefore limited. It will not help to try to imagine that one has webbing on one's arms, which enables one to fly around at dusk and dawn catching insects in one's mouth; that one has very poor vision, and perceives the surrounding world by a system of reflected high-frequency sound signals; and that one spends the day hanging upside down by one's feet in an attic. In so far as I can imagine this (which is not very far), it tells me only what it would be like for *me* to behave as a bat behaves. But that is not the question. I want to know what it is like for a *bat* to be a bat. Yet if I try to imagine this, I am restricted to the resources of my own mind, and those resources are inadequate to the task. I cannot perform it either by imagining additions to my present experience, or by imagining segments gradually subtracted from it, or by imagining some combination of additions, subtractions, and modifications.

To the extent that I could look and behave like a wasp or a bat without changing my fundamental structure, my experiences would not be anything like the experiences of those animals. On the other hand, it is doubtful that any meaning can be attached to the supposition that I should possess the internal neurophysiological constitution of a bat. Even if I could by gradual degrees be transformed into a bat, nothing in my present constitution enables me to imagine what the experiences of such a future stage of myself thus metamorphosed would be like. The best evidence would come from the experiences of bats, if we only knew what they were like.

So if extrapolation from our own case is involved in the idea of what it is like to be a bat, the extrapolation must be incompletable. We cannot form more than a schematic conception of what it *is* like. For example, we may ascribe general *types* of experience on the basis of the animal's structure and behaviour. Thus we describe bat sonar as a form of three-dimensional forward perception; we believe that bats feel some versions of pain, fear, hunger, and lust, and that they have other, more familiar *types* of perception besides sonar. But we believe that these experiences also have in each case a specific subjective character, which it is beyond our ability to conceive. And if there's conscious life elsewhere in the universe, it is likely that some of it will not be describable even in the most general experiential terms available to us[2]. (The problem is not confined to exotic cases, however, for it exists between one person and another. The subjective character of the experience of a person deaf and blind from birth is not accessible to me, for example, nor presumably is mine to him. This does not prevent us each from believing that the other's experience has such a subjective character.)

If anyone is inclined to deny that we can believe in the existence of facts like this whose exact nature we cannot possibly conceive, he should reflect that in contemplating the bats we are in much the same position that intelligent bats or Martians[3] would occupy if they tried to form a conception of what it was like to be us. The structure of their own minds might make it impossible for them to succeed, but we know they would be wrong to conclude that there is not anything precise that it is like to be us: that only certain general types of mental state could be ascribed to us (perhaps perception and appetite would be concepts common to us both; perhaps not). We know they would be wrong to draw such a sceptical conclusion because we know what it is like to be us. And we know that while it includes an enormous amount of variation and complexity, and while we do not possess the vocabulary to describe it adequately, its subjective character is highly specific, and in some respects describable in terms that can be understood only by creatures like us. The fact that we cannot expect ever to accommodate in our language a detailed description of Martian or bat phenomenology should not lead us to dismiss as meaningless the claim that bats and Martians have experiences fully comparable in richness of detail to our own. It would be fine if someone were to develop concepts and a theory that enabled us to think about those things; but such an understanding may be permanently denied to us by the limits of our nature. And to deny the reality or logical significance of what we can never describe or understand is the crudest form of cognitive dissonance.

1 By 'our own case' I do not mean just 'my own case,' but rather the mentalistic ideas that we apply unproblematically to ourselves and other human beings.
2 Therefore the analogical form of the English expression 'what it is *like*' is misleading. It does not mean 'what (in our experience) it *resembles*,' but rather 'how it is for the subject himself.'
3 Any intelligent extraterrestrial beings totally different from us.

'What a Strange Nature Is Knowledge!'
Mary Wollstonecraft Shelley, 1818

When the man-made 'monster' in Mary Shelley's (1797–1851) *Frankenstein* acquires knowledge and an awareness of self he is delighted, but irreversibly pained.

My days were spent in close attention, that I might more speedily master the language; and I may boast that I improved more rapidly than the Arabian, who understood very little and conversed in broken accents, whilst I comprehended and could imitate almost every word that was spoken.

While I improved in speech, I also learned the science of letters, as it was taught to the stranger; and this opened before me a wide field for wonder and delight.

The book from which Felix instructed Safie was Volney's *Ruins of Empires*. I should not have understood the purport of this book had not Felix, in reading it, given very minute explanations. He had chosen this work, he said, because the declamatory style was framed in imitation of the Eastern authors. Through this work I obtained a cursory knowledge of history and a view of the several empires at present existing in the world; it gave me an insight into the manners, governments, and religions of the different nations of the earth. I heard of the slothful Asiatics; of the stupendous genius and mental activity of the Grecians; of the wars and wonderful virtue of the early Romans – of their subsequent degeneration – of the decline of that mighty empire; of chivalry; Christianity, and kings. I heard of the discovery of the American hemisphere and wept with Safie over the hapless fate of its original inhabitants.

These wonderful narrations inspired me with strange feelings. Was man, indeed, at once so powerful, so virtuous, and magnificent, yet so vicious and base? He appeared at one

AWARENESS OF SELF

23

time a mere scion of the evil principle, and at another as all that can be conceived of noble and godlike. To be a great and virtuous man appeared the highest honour that can befall a sensitive being; to be base and vicious, as many on record have been, appeared the lowest degradation, a condition more abject than that of the blind mole or harmless worm. For a long time I could not conceive how one man could go forth to murder his fellow, or even why there were laws and governments; but when I heard details of vice and bloodshed, my wonder ceased, and I turned away with disgust and loathing.

Every conversation of the cottagers now opened new wonders to me. While I listened to the instructions which Felix bestowed upon the Arabian, the strange system of human society was explained to me. I heard of the division of property, of immense wealth and squalid poverty; of rank, descent, and noble blood.

The words induced me to turn towards myself. I learned that the possessions most esteemed by your fellow creatures were high and unsullied descent united with riches. A man might be respected with only one of these acquisitions, but without either he was considered, except in very rare instances, as a vagabond and a slave, doomed to waste his powers for the profits of the chosen few. And what was I? Of my creation and creator I was absolutely ignorant; but I knew that I possessed no money, no friends, no kind of property. I was, besides, endowed with a figure hideously deformed and loathsome; I was not even of the same nature as man. I was more agile than they and could subsist upon coarser diet; I bore the extremes of heat and cold with less injury to my frame; my stature far exceeded theirs. When I looked around, I saw and heard of none like me. Was I then a monster, a blot upon the earth, from which all men fled, and whom all men disowned?

I cannot describe to you the agony that these reflections inflicted upon me; I tried to dispel them, but sorrow only increased with knowledge. Oh, that I had for ever remained in my native wood, nor known nor felt beyond the sensations of hunger, thirst, and heat!

Of what a strange nature is knowledge! It clings to the mind when it has once seized on it, like a lichen on the rock. I wished sometimes to shake off all thought and feeling, but I learned that there was but one means to overcome the sensation of pain, and that was death – a state which I feared yet did not understand. I admired virtue and good feelings, and loved the gentle manners and amiable qualities of my cottagers; but I was shut out from intercourse with them, except through means which I obtained by stealth, when I was unseen and unknown, and which rather increased than satisfied the desire I had of becoming one among my fellows. The gentle words of Agatha, and the animated smiles of the charming Arabian, were not for me. The mild exhortations of the old man, and the lively conversation of the loved Felix, were not for me. Miserable, unhappy wretch!

Other lessons were impressed upon me even more deeply. I heard of the difference of sexes; the birth and growth of children; how the father doted on the smiles of the infant, and the lively sallies of the older child; how all the life and cares of the mother were wrapt up in the precious charge; how the mind of youth expanded and gained knowledge; of brother, sister, and all the various relationships which bind one human being to another in mutual bonds.

But where were my friends and relations? No father had watched my infant days, no mother had blessed me with smiles and caresses; or if they had, all my past life was now a blot, a blind vacancy in which I distinguished nothing. From my earliest remembrance I had been as I then was in height and proportion. I had never yet seen a being resembling me, or who claimed any intercourse with me. What was I? The question again recurred, to be answered only with groans.

'Superadded Consciousness'
George Eliot, 1859

> The narrator of George Eliot's (1819–1880) novella *The Lifted Veil* experiences visions when he falls seriously ill. His "superadded consciousness" is both wearying and upsetting.

Suddenly I was conscious that my father was in the room, but not alone: there were two persons with him. Strange! I had heard no footstep, I had not seen the door open; but I saw my father, and at his right hand our neighbour Mrs Filmore, whom I remembered very well, though I had not seen her for five years. She was a commonplace middle-aged woman, in silk and cashmere; but the lady on the left of my father was not more than twenty, a tall, slim, willowy figure, with luxuriant blond hair, arranged in cunning braids and folds that looked almost too massive for the slight figure and the small-featured, thin-lipped face they crowned. But the face had not a girlish expression: the features were sharp, the pale grey eyes at once acute, restless, and sarcastic. They were fixed on me in half-smiling curiosity, and I felt a painful sensation as if a sharp wind were cutting me. The pale-green dress, and the green leaves that seemed to form a border about her pale blond hair, made me think of a Water-Nixie – for my mind was full of German lyrics, and this pale, fatal-eyed woman, with the green weeds, looked like a birth from some cold sedgy stream, the daughter of an aged river.

"Well, Latimer, you thought me long," my father said ...

But while the last word was in my ears, the whole group vanished, and there was nothing between me and the Chinese printed folding-screen that stood before the door. I was cold and trembling; I could only totter forward and throw myself on the sofa. This strange new power had manifested itself again ...

But *was* it a power? Might it not rather be a disease – a sort of intermittent delirium, concentrating my energy of brain into moments of unhealthy activity, and leaving my saner hours all the more barren? I felt a dizzy sense of unreality in what my eye rested on; I grasped the bell convulsively, like one trying to free himself from nightmare, and rang it twice. Pierre came with a look of alarm in his face.

"Monsieur ne se trouve pas bien?" he said anxiously.

"I'm tired of waiting, Pierre," I said, as distinctly and emphatically as I could, like a man determined to be sober in spite of wine; "I'm afraid something has happened to my father – he's usually so punctual. Run to the Hôtel des Bergues and see if he is there."

Pierre left the room at once, with a soothing "Bien, Monsieur"; and I felt the better for this scene of simple, waking prose. Seeking to calm myself still further, I went into my bedroom, adjoining the *salon*, and opened a case of eau-de-Cologne; took out a bottle; went through the process of taking out the cork very neatly, and then rubbed the reviving spirit over my hands and forehead, and under my nostrils, drawing a new delight from the scent because I had procured it by slow details of labour, and by no strange sudden madness. Already I had begun to taste something of the horror that belongs to the lot of a human being whose nature is not adjusted to simple human conditions.

Still enjoying the scent, I returned to the *salon*, but it was not unoccupied, as it had been before I left it. In front of the Chinese folding-screen there was my father, with Mrs Filmore on his right hand, and on his left – the slim, blond-haired girl, with the keen face and the keen eyes fixed on me in half-smiling curiosity.

"Well, Latimer, you thought me long," my father said…

I heard no more, felt no more, till I became conscious that I was lying with my head low on the sofa, Pierre, and my father

by my side. As soon as I was thoroughly revived, my father left
the room, and presently returned, saying –

"I've been to tell the ladies how you are, Latimer. They
were waiting in the next room. We shall put off our shopping
expedition to-day."

Presently he said, "That young lady is Bertha Grant, Mrs
Filmore's orphan niece. Filmore has adopted her, and she lives
with them, so you will have her for a neighbour when we go
home – perhaps for a near relation; for there is a tenderness
between her and Alfred, I suspect, and I should be gratified by
the match, since Filmore means to provide for her in every way
as if she were his daughter. It had not occurred to me that you
knew nothing about her living with the Filmores."

He made no further allusion to the fact of my having
fainted at the moment of seeing her, and I would not for the
world have told him the reason: I shrank from the idea of
disclosing to any one what might be regarded as a pitiable
peculiarity, most of all from betraying it to my father, who
would have suspected my sanity ever after.

I do not mean to dwell with particularity on the details of
my experience. I have described these two cases at length,
because they had definite, clearly traceable results in my
after-lot.

Shortly after this last occurrence – I think the very next day
– I began to be aware of a phase in my abnormal sensibility, to
which, from the languid and slight nature of my intercourse
with others since my illness, I had not been alive before. This
was the obtrusion on my mind of the mental process going
forward in first one person, and then another, with whom I
happened to be in contact: the vagrant, frivolous ideas and
emotions of some uninteresting acquaintance – Mrs Filmore,
for example – would force themselves on my consciousness
like an importunate, ill-played musical instrument, or the
loud activity of an imprisoned insect. But this unpleasant

sensibility was fitful, and left me moments of rest, when the souls of my companions were once more shut out from me, and I felt a relief such as silence brings to wearied nerves. I might have believed this importunate insight to be merely a diseased activity of the imagination, but that my prevision of incalculable words and actions proved it to have a fixed relation to the mental process in other minds. But this superadded consciousness, wearying and annoying enough when it urged on me the trivial experience of indifferent people, became an intense pain and grief when it seemed to be opening to me the souls of those who were in a close relation to me – when the rational talk, the graceful attentions, the wittily-turned phrases, and the kindly deeds, which used to make the web of their characters, were seen as if thrust asunder by a microscopic vision, that showed all the intermediate frivolities, all the suppressed egoism, all the struggling chaos of puerilities, meanness, vague capricious memories, and indolent make-shift thoughts, from which human words and deeds emerge like leaflets covering a fermenting heap.

Antechamber of Consciousness
Francis Galton, 1883

> English scientist and statistician Francis Galton (1822–1911) identified different 'chambers' of consciousness in these writings about the development of ideas.

When I am engaged in trying to think anything out, the process of doing so appears to me to be this: The ideas that lie at any moment within my full consciousness seem to attract of their own accord the most appropriate out of a number of other ideas that are lying close at hand, but imperfectly within the range of my consciousness. There seems to be a presence-chamber in my mind where full consciousness holds court, and where two or three ideas are at the same time in audience, and an antechamber full of more or less allied ideas, which is situated just beyond the full ken of consciousness. Out of this antechamber the ideas most nearly allied to those in the presence-chamber appear to be summoned in a mechanically logical way, and to have their turn of audience.

The successful progress of thought appears to depend – first, on a large attendance in the antechamber; secondly, on the presence there of no ideas except such as are strictly germane to the topic under consideration; thirdly, on the justness of the logical mechanism that issues the summons. The thronging of the antechamber is, I am convinced, altogether beyond my control; if the ideas do not appear, I cannot create them, nor compel them to come. The exclusion of alien ideas is accompanied by a sense of mental effort and volition whenever the topic under consideration is unattractive, otherwise it proceeds automatically, for if an intruding idea finds nothing to cling to, it is unable to hold its place in the antechamber, and slides back again. An animal absorbed in a favourite occupation shows no sign of painful effort of attention; on the contrary, he resents interruption that solicits his attention elsewhere.

The consequence of all this is that the mind frequently does good work without the slightest exertion. In composition it will often produce a better effect than if it acted with effort, because the essence of good composition is that the ideas should be connected by the easiest possible transitions. When a man has been thinking hard and long upon a subject, he becomes temporarily familiar with certain steps of thought, certain short cuts, and certain far-fetched associations, that do not commend themselves to the minds of other persons, nor indeed to his own at other times; therefore, it is better that his transitory familiarity with them should have come to an end before he begins to write or speak. When he returns to the work after a sufficient pause he is conscious that his ideas have settled; that is, they have lost their adventitious relations to one another, and stand in those in which they are likely to reside permanently in his own mind, and to exist in the minds of others.

Although the brain is able to do very fair work fluently in an automatic way, and though it will of its own accord strike out sudden and happy ideas, it is questionable if it is capable of working thoroughly and profoundly without past or present effort. The character of this effort seems to me chiefly to lie in bringing the contents of the antechamber more nearly within the ken of consciousness, which then takes comprehensive note of all its contents, and compels the logical faculty to test them *seriatum* before selecting the fittest for a summons to the presence-chamber.

Extreme fluency and a vivid and rapid imagination are gifts naturally and healthfully possessed by those who rise to be great orators or literary men, for they could not have become successful in those careers without it. The curious fact already alluded to of five editors of newspapers being known to me as having phantasmagoria, points to a connection between two forms of fluency, the literary and the visual. Fluency may be also a morbid faculty, being markedly increased by alcohol (as poets are never tired of telling us), and by various drugs; and it exists in delirium, insanity, and states of high emotions. The fluency of a vulgar scold is extraordinary.

In preparing to write or speak upon a subject of which the details have been mastered, I gather, after some inquiry, that the usual method among persons who have the gift of fluency is to think cursorily on topics connected with it, until what I have called the antechamber is well filled with cognate ideas. Then, to allow the ideas to link themselves in their own way, breaking the linkage continually and recommencing afresh until some line of thought has suggested itself that appears from a rapid and light glance to thread the chief topics together. After this the connections are brought step by step fully into consciousness, they are short-circuited here and extended there, as found advisable, until a firm connection is found to be established between all parts of the subject. After this is done the mental effort is over, and the composition may proceed fluently in an automatic way. Though this, I believe, is a usual way, it is by no means universal, for there are very great differences in the conditions under which different persons compose most readily. They seem to afford as good evidence of the variety of mental and bodily constitutions as can be met with in any other line of inquiry.

'The Perfect Combination'
De Mirjian Studios, c.1929

For Marguerite Agniel, who adopted this Buddha pose in her book *The Art of the Body*, the perfect combination of body and mind was an outcome of – and an aid to – deep thought.

'Teletransportation'
Derek Parfit, 1984

> In his first book, *Reasons and Persons*, British philosopher
> Derek Parfit (b. 1942) argued there is no unique 'self'.
> These two excerpts feature in the chapter 'What we believe
> ourselves to be'.

I enter the Teletransporter. I have been to Mars before, but only
by the old method, a space-ship journey taking several weeks.
This machine will send me at the speed of light. I merely have
to press the green button. Like others, I am nervous. Will it
work? I remind myself what I have been told to expect. When
I press the button, I shall lose consciousness, and then wake
up at what seems a moment later. In fact I shall have been
unconscious for about an hour. The Scanner here on Earth will
destroy my brain and body, while recording the exact states of
all of my cells. It will then transmit this information by radio.
Travelling at the speed of light, the message will take three
minutes to reach the Replicator on Mars. This will then create,
out of new matter, a brain and body exactly like mine. It will be
in this body that I shall wake up.

Though I believe that this is what will happen, I still
hesitate. But then I remember seeing my wife grin when, at
breakfast today, I revealed my nervousness. As she reminded
me, she has been often teletransported, and there is nothing
wrong with *her*. I press the button. As predicted, I lose and
seem at once to regain consciousness, but in a different
cubicle. Examining my new body, I find no change at all. Even
the cut on my upper lip, from this morning's shave, is still
there.

Several years pass, during which I am often Teletransported. I am now back in the cubicle, ready for another trip to
Mars. But this time, when I press the green button, I do not

lose consciousness. There is a whirring soun[...]
leave the cubicle, and say to the attendant: "It[...]
What did I do wrong?"

"It's working," he replies, handing me a p[...]
This reads: 'The New Scanner records your blu[...] ...without
destroying your brain and body. We hope that you will welcome
the opportunities which this technical advance offers.'

The attendant tells me that I am one of the first people to
use the New Scanner. He adds that, if I stay for an hour, I can
use the Intercom to see and talk to myself on Mars.

"Wait a minute," I reply. "If I'm here I can't *also* be
on Mars."

Someone politely coughs, a white-coated man who asks
to speak to me in private. We go to his office, here he tells
me to sit down, and pauses. Then he says: "I'm afraid that
we're having problems with the New Scanner. It records your
blueprint just as accurately, as you will see when you talk to
yourself on Mars. But it seems to be damaging the cardiac
systems which it scans. Judging from the results so far, though
you will be quite healthy on Mars, here on Earth you must
expect cardiac failure within the next few days."

The attendant later calls me to the Intercom. On the screen
I see myself just as I do in the mirror every morning. But there
are two differences. On the screen I am not left–right reversed.
And, while I stand here speechless, I can see and hear myself,
in the studio on Mars, starting to speak.

...

Simple Teletransportation and the Branch-Line Case
At the beginning of my story, the Scanner destroys my brain
and body. My blueprint is beamed to Mars, where another
machine makes an organic *Replica* of me. My Replica thinks
that he is me, and he seems to remember living my life up to
the moment when I pressed the green button. In every other
way, both physically and psychologically, we are exactly similar.

returned to Earth, everyone would think that he was me.

Simple Teletransportation, as just described, is a common feature in science fiction. And it is believed, by some readers of this fiction, merely to be the fastest way of travelling. They believe that my Replica *would* be *me*. Other science fiction readers, and some of the characters in this fiction, take a different view. They believe that, when I press the green button, I die. My Replica is *someone else*, who has been made to be exactly like me.

This second view seems to be supported by the end of my story. The New Scanner does not destroy my brain and body. Besides gathering the information, it merely damages my heart. While I am in the cubicle, with the green button pressed, nothing seems to happen. I walk out, and learn that in a few days I shall die. I later talk, by two-way television, to my Replica on Mars. Let us continue the story. Since my Replica knows that I am about to die, he tries to console me with the same thoughts with which I recently tried to console a dying friend. It is sad to learn, on the receiving end, how uncon-soling these thoughts are. My Replica then assures me that he will take up my life where I leave off. He loves my wife, and together they will care for my children. And he will finish the book that I am writing. Besides having all of my drafts, he has all of my intentions. I must admit that he can finish my book as well as I could. All these facts console me a little. Dying when I know that I shall have a Replica is not quite as bad as, simply, dying. Even so, I shall soon lose consciousness, forever.

In Simple Teletransportation, I am destroyed before I am Replicated. This makes it easier to believe that this *is* a way of travelling – that my Replica *is* me. At the end of my story, my life and that of my Replica overlap. Call this the *Branch-Line Case*. In this case, I cannot hope to travel on the *Main Line*, waking up on Mars with forty years of life ahead. I shall stay on the Branch-Line, here on earth, which ends a few days later.

Since I can talk to my Replica, it seems clear that he is *not* me. Though he is exactly like me, he is one person, and I am another. When I pinch myself, he feels nothing. When I have my heart attack, he will again feel nothing. And when I am dead he will live for another forty years.

If we believe that my Replica is not me, it is natural to assume that my prospect, on the Branch Line, is almost as bad as ordinary death. I shall deny this assumption. As I shall argue later, being destroyed and Replicated is about as good as ordinary survival. I can best defend this claim, and the wider view of which it is part, after discussing the past debate about personal identity.

Qualitative and numerical identity

There are two kinds of sameness, or identity. I and my Replica are *qualitatively identical*, or exactly alike. But we may not be *numerically identical*, or one and the same person. Similarly, two white billiard balls are not numerically but may be qualitatively identical. If I paint one of these balls red, it will cease to be qualitatively identical with itself as it was. But the red ball that I later see and the white ball that I painted red are numerically identical. They are one and the same ball.

We might say, of someone, "After his accident, he is no longer the same person". This is a claim about both kinds of identity. We claim that *he*, the same person, is *not* now the same person. This is not a contradiction. We merely mean that this person's character has changed. This numerically identical person is now qualitatively different.

When we are concerned about our future, it is our numerical identity that we are concerned about. I may believe that, after my marriage, I shall not be the same person. But this does not make marriage death. However much I change, I shall still be alive if there will be some person living who will *be* me.

Though our chief concern is our numerical identity, psychological changes matter. Indeed, on one view, certain kinds of qualitative change destroy numerical identity. If certain things happen to me, the truth might not be that I become a very different person. The truth might be that I cease to exist – that the resulting person is someone else.

A Grand Transformation Scene
F Anstey, 1882

In the second chapter of F Anstey's (1856–1934) comic novel *Vice Versâ*, Paul Bultitude refuses his son Dick's request to change schools. Bultitude's wishful response has confusing consequences.

"Perhaps you will believe me," [Paul Bultitude] said, impressively, "when I tell you, old as I am and much as you envy me, I only wish, at this very moment, I could be a boy again, like you. Going back to school wouldn't make me unhappy, I can tell you."

It is so fatally easy to say more than we mean in the desire to make as strong an impression as possible. Well for most of us that – more fortunate than Mr Bultitude – we can generally do so without fear of being taken too strictly at our word.

As he spoke these unlucky words, he felt a slight shiver, followed by a curious shrinking sensation all over him. It was odd, too, but the arm-chair in which he sat seemed to have grown so much bigger all at once. He felt a passing surprise, but concluded it must be fancy, and went on as comfortably as before.

"I should like it, my boy, but what's the good of wishing? I only mention it to prove that I was not speaking at random. I'm an old man and you're a young boy, and, that being so, why, of course – What the dooce are you giggling about?"

For Dick, after some seconds of half-frightened open-mouthed staring, had suddenly burst into a violent fit of almost hysterical giggling, which he seemed trying vainly to suppress.

This naturally annoyed Mr Bultitude, and he went on with immense dignity, "I, ah, I'm not aware that I've been saying anything particularly ridiculous. You seem to be amused?"

"Don't!" gasped Dick. "It, it isn't anything you're saying – it's, it's – oh, can't you feel any difference?"

"The sooner you go back to school the better!" said Paul angrily. "I wash my hands of you. When I do take the trouble to give you any advice, it's received with ridicule. You always were an ill-mannered little cub. I've had quite enough of this. Leave the room, sir!"

The wheels must have belonged to some other cab, for none had stopped at the pavement as yet; but Mr Bultitude was justly indignant, and could stand the interview no longer. Dick, however, made no attempt to move; he remained there, choking and shaking with laughter, while his father sat stiffly on his chair, trying to ignore his son's unmannerly conduct, but only partially succeeding.

No one can calmly endure watching other people laughing at him like idiots, while he is left perfectly incapable of guessing what he has said or done to amuse them. Even when this is known, it requires a peculiarly keen sense of humour to see the point of a joke against oneself.

At last his patience gave out, and he said coldly, "Now, perhaps, if you are quite yourself again, you will be good enough to let me know what the joke is?"

Dick, looking flushed and half-ashamed, tried again and again to speak, but each time the attempt was too much for him. After a time he did succeed, but his voice was hoarse and shaken with laughter as he spoke. "Haven't you found it out yet? Go and look at yourself in the glass – it will make you roar!"

There was the usual narrow sheet of plate glass at the back of the sideboard, and to this Mr Bultitude walked, almost under protest, and with a cold dignity. It occurred to him that he might have a smudge on his face or something wrong with his collar and tie – something to account to some extent for his son's frivolous and insulting behaviour. No suspicion of the terrible truth crossed his mind as yet.

Meanwhile Dick was looking on eagerly with a chuckle of anticipation, as one who watches the dawning appreciation of an excellent joke.

But no sooner had Paul met the reflection in the glass than he started back in incredulous horror – then returned and stared again and again.

Surely, surely, this could not be he!

He had expected to see his own familiar portly bow-windowed presence there – but somehow, look as he would, the mirror insisted upon reflecting the figure of his son Dick. Could he possibly have become invisible and have lost the power of casting a reflection – or how was it that Dick, and only Dick, was to be seen there?

How was it, too, when he looked round, there was the boy still sitting there. It could not be Dick, evidently, that he saw in the glass. Besides, the reflection opposite him moved when he moved, returned when he returned, copied his every gesture!

He turned round upon his son with angry and yet hopeful suspicion. "You, you've been playing some of your infernal tricks with this mirror, sir," he cried fiercely. "What have you done to it?"

"Done! How could I do anything to it? As if you didn't know that!"

"Then," stammered Paul, determined to know the worst, "then do you, do you mean to tell me you can see any

– alteration in me? Tell me the truth now!"

"I should just think I could!" said Dick emphatically. "It's very queer, but just look here," and he came up to the sideboard and placed himself by the side of his horrified father. "Why," he said, with another giggle, "we're – he-he – as like as two peas!"

They were indeed; the glass reflected now two small boys, each with chubby cheeks and fair hair, both dressed, too, exactly alike, in Eton jackets and broad white collars; the only difference to be seen between them was that, while one face wore an expression of intense glee and satisfaction, the other – the one which Mr Bultitude was beginning to fear must belong to him – was lengthened and drawn with dismay and bewilderment.

"Dick," said Paul faintly, "what is all this? Who has been, been taking these liberties with me?"

"I'm sure I don't know," protested Dick. "It wasn't me. I believe you did it all yourself."

"Did it all myself!" repeated Paul indignantly. "Is it likely I should? It's some trickery, I tell you, some villainous plot. The worst of it is," he added plaintively, "I don't understand who I'm supposed to be now. Dick, who am I?"

"You can't be me," said Dick authoritatively, "because here I am, you know. And you're not yourself, that's very plain. You must be somebody, I suppose," he added dubiously.

'Thou Splendid, Heavenly Lady!'
E T W Hoffman, 1817

> In E T W Hoffman's (1776–1822) *The Sandman* young
> university student Nathaniel becomes infatuated with
> Olympia and attends her father's party in order to meet
> her. He, alone, imbues her stiff and lifeless form with
> consciousness.

Nathaniel found a card of invitation, and with heart beating
highly went at the appointed hour to the professor's, where the
coaches were already rolling, and the lights were shining in the
decorated saloons. The company was numerous and brilliant.
Olympia appeared dressed with great richness and taste. Her
beautifully turned face, her figure called for admiration. The
somewhat strange bend of her back inwards, the wasp-like
thinness of her waist, seemed to be produced by too tight lacing.
In her step and deportment there was something measured
and stiff, which struck many as unpleasant, but it was ascribed
to the constraint produced by the company. The concert began,
Olympia played the piano with great dexterity, and executed a
bravura, with a voice, like the sound of a glass bell, clear, and
almost cutting. Nathaniel was quite enraptured; he stood in the
hindermost row, and could not perfectly recognise Olympia's
features in the dazzling light. He, therefore, quite unperceived,
took out Coppola's glass, and looked towards the fair Olympia.
Ah! then he saw, with what a longing glance she looked towards
him, how every tone first resolved itself plainly in the glance of
love, which penetrated, in its glowing career, his inmost soul.
The artistical *roulades* seemed to Nathaniel the exultation of a
mind illuminated with love, and when, at last, after the cadence,
the long trill sounded shrilly through the saloon, he felt as if
grasped by glowing arms; he could no longer restrain himself,
but with mingled pain and rapture shouted out, "Olympia!"

All looked at him, and many laughed. The organist of the cathedral made a more gloomy face than usual, and simply said: "Well, well." The concert had finished, the ball began. "To dance with her – with her!" That was the aim of all Nathaniel's wishes, of all his efforts; but how to gain courage to ask her, the queen of the festival? Nevertheless – he himself did not know how it happened – no sooner had the dancing begun, than he was standing close to Olympia, who had not yet been asked to dance, and, scarcely able to stammer out a few words, had seized her hand. The hand of Olympia was as cold as ice; he felt a horrible deadly frost thrilling through him. He looked into her eye – that was beaming full of love and desire, and at the same time it seemed as though the pulse began to beat, and the stream of life to glow in the cold hand. And in the soul of Nathaniel the joy of love rose still higher; he clasped the beautiful Olympia, and with her flew through the dance. He thought that his dancing was usually correct as to time, but the peculiar rhythmical steadiness with which Olympia moved, and which often put him completely out, soon showed him, that his time was very defective. However, he would dance with no other lady, and would have liked to murder any one who approached Olympia for the purpose of asking her. But this only happened twice, and to his astonishment Olympia remained seated after every dance, when he lost no time in making her rise again. Had he been able to see any other object besides the fair Olympia, all sorts of unfortunate quarrels would have been inevitable, for the half-soft, scarcely-suppressed laughter, which arose among the young people in every corner, was manifestly directed to Olympia, whom they pursued with very curious glances – one could not tell why. Heated by the dance, and by the wine, of which he had freely partaken, Nathaniel had laid aside all his ordinary reserve. He sat by Olympia, with her hand in his, and, highly inflamed and inspired, told his passion, in words which no one understood

– neither himself nor Olympia. Yet, perhaps, *she* did; for she looked immoveably in his face, and sighed several times, "Ah, ah!" Upon this, Nathaniel said, "Oh, thou splendid, heavenly lady! Thou ray from the promised land of love – thou deep soul, in which all my being is reflected!" with much more stuff of the like kind; but Olympia merely went on sighing, "Ah – ah!" Professor Spalanzani occasionally passed the happy pair, and smiled on them, with a look of singular satisfaction. To Nathaniel, although he felt in quite another region, it seemed all at once as though Professor Spalanzani was growing considerably darker; he looked around, and, to his no small horror, perceived that the two last candles in the empty saloon had burned down to their sockets, and were just going out. Music and dancing had ceased long ago. "Separation – separation!" he cried, wildly, and in despair; he kissed Olympia's hand, he bent towards her mouth, when his glowing lips were met by lips cold as ice! Just as when he touched Olympia's cold hand, he felt himself overcome by horror; the legend of the dead bride darted suddenly through his mind, but Olympia pressed him fast, and her lips seemed to recover to life at his kiss. Professor Spalanzani strode through the empty hall, his steps caused a hollow echo, and his figure, round which a flickering shadow played, had a fearful, spectral appearance. "Dost thou love me, dost thou love me, Olympia? Only this word! – Dost thou love me?" So whispered Nathaniel; but Olympia, as she rose, only sighed, "Ah – ah!" "Yes, my gracious, my beautiful star of love," said Nathaniel, "thou hast risen upon me, and thou wilt shine, ever illuminating my inmost soul." "Ah – ah!" replied Olympia, going. Nathaniel followed her; they both stood before the professor.

"You have had a very animated conversation with my daughter," said he, smiling; "so, dear Herr Nathaniel, if you have any taste for talking with a silly girl, your visits shall be welcome."

Nathaniel departed, with a whole heaven beaming in his bosom. The next day Spalanzani's festival was the subject of conversation. Notwithstanding the professor had done every thing to appear splendid, the wags had all sorts of incongruities and oddities to talk about, and were particularly hard upon the dumb, stiff Olympia, to whom, in spite of her beautiful exterior, they ascribed absolute stupidity, and were pleased to find therein the cause why Spalanzani kept her so long concealed. Nathaniel did not hear this without increased rage; but, nevertheless, he held his peace, for, thought he, "Is it worth while to convince these fellows that it is their own stupidity that prevents them from recognising Olympia's deep, noble mind?"

One day Sigismund said to him: "Be kind enough, brother, to tell me how it was possible for a sensible fellow like you to fall in love with that wax face, that wooden doll up there?"

Nathaniel was about to fly out in a passion, but he quickly recollected himself, and retorted: "Tell me, Sigismund, how it is that Olympia's heavenly charms could escape your glance, which generally perceives every thing so clearly – your active senses? But, for that very reason, Heaven be thanked, I have not you for my rival; otherwise, one of us must have fallen a bleeding corpse!"

Sigismund plainly perceived his friend's condition, so he skilfully gave the conversation a turn, and added, after observing that in love-affairs there was no disputing about the object: "Nevertheless it is strange, that many of us think much the same about Olympia. To us – pray do not take it ill, brother, – she appears singularly stiff and soulless. Her shape is symmetrical – so is her face – that is true! She might pass for beautiful, if her glance were not so utterly without a ray of life – without the power of seeing. Her pace is strangely measured, every movement seems to depend on some wound-up clock-work. Her playing – her singing has the unpleasantly correct and spiritless measure of a singing machine, and the same may be said of her dancing. To us, this Olympia has been quite unpleasant; we wished to have nothing to do with her; it seems as if she acts like a living being, and yet has some strange peculiarity of her own." Nathaniel did not completely yield to the bitter feeling, which was coming over him at these words of Sigismund; he mastered his indignation, and merely said, with great earnestness, "Well may Olympia appear awful to you, cold prosaic man. Only to the poetical mind does the similarly organised develop itself. To me alone was her glance of love revealed, beaming through mind and thought; only in the love of Olympia do I find myself again. It may not suit you, that she does not indulge in idle chit-chat like other shallow minds. She utters few words, it is true, but these few words appear as genuine hieroglyphics of the inner world, full of love and deep knowledge of the spiritual life in contemplation of the eternal *yonder*. But you have no sense for all this, and my words are wasted on you."

Humanoid Robot
Dianne Harris, 2002

Robots with uncanny human features prompt questions about artificial consciousness and the possibility of uploading human minds to machines. Artist Dianne Harris (b. 1969), founding director and curator of the Kinetica Museum, describes her work as "exploring the unseen realms of existence".

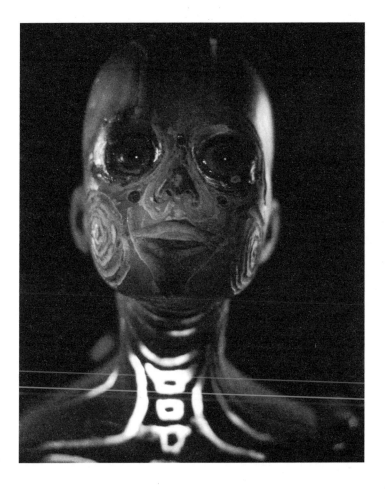

ARTIFICIAL CONSCIOUSNESS

'Opinions Opposed to My Own'
Alan Turing, 1950

> In 1950, British mathematician Alan Turing (1912–1954)
> predicted that the concept of thinking machines would be
> unremarkable by the year 2000. In this excerpt from a paper
> published in the journal *Mind* Turing tackles some of the
> counterarguments to this view.

These arguments take the form 'I grant you that you can make
machines do all the things you have mentioned but you will
never be able to make one to do X.' Numerous features X are
suggested in this connexion. I offer a selection:

> Be kind, resourceful, beautiful, friendly, have initiative,
> have a sense of humour, tell right from wrong, make
> mistakes, fall in love, enjoy strawberries and cream,
> make some one fall in love with it, learn from experience,
> use words properly, be the subject of its own thought,
> have as much diversity of behaviour as a man, do
> something really new.

No support is usually offered for these statements. I believe
they are mostly founded on the principle of scientific induction. A man has seen thousands of machines in his lifetime.
From what he sees of them he draws a number of general
conclusions. They are ugly, each is designed for a very limited
purpose, when required for a minutely different purpose
they are useless, the variety of behaviour of any one of them
is very small, etc., etc. Naturally he concludes that these are
necessary properties of machines in general. Many of these
limitations are associated with the very small storage capacity
of most machines. (I am assuming that the idea of storage
capacity is extended in some way to cover machines other

than discrete-state machines. The exact definition does not matter as no mathematical accuracy is claimed in the present discussion.) A few years ago, when very little had been heard of digital computers, it was possible to elicit much incredulity concerning them, if one mentioned their properties without describing their construction. That was presumably due to a similar application of the principle of scientific induction. These applications of the principle are of course largely unconscious. When a burnt child fears the fire and shows that he fears it by avoiding it, I should say that he was applying scientific induction. (I could of course also describe his behaviour in many other ways.) The works and customs of mankind do not seem to be very suitable material to which to apply scientific induction. A very large part of space–time must be investigated, if reliable results are to be obtained. Otherwise we may (as most English children do) decide that everybody speaks English, and that it is silly to learn French.

There are, however, special remarks to be made about many of the disabilities that have been mentioned. The inability to enjoy strawberries and cream may have struck the reader as frivolous. Possibly a machine might be made to enjoy this delicious dish, but any attempt to make one do so would be idiotic. What is important about this disability is that it contributes to some of the other disabilities, e.g. to the difficulty of the same kind of friendliness occurring between man and machine as between white man and white man, or between black man and black man.

The claim that 'machines cannot make mistakes' seems a curious one. One is tempted to retort, 'Are they any the worse for that?' But let us adopt a more sympathetic attitude, and try to see what is really meant. I think this criticism can be explained in terms of the imitation game. It is claimed that the interrogator could distinguish the machine from the man simply by setting them a number of problems in arithmetic. The machine would be unmasked because of its deadly accuracy. The reply to this is simple. The machine (programmed for playing the game) would not attempt to give the right answers to the arithmetic problems. It would deliberately introduce mistakes in a manner calculated to confuse the interrogator. A mechanical fault would probably show itself through an unsuitable decision as to what sort of a mistake to make in the arithmetic. Even this interpretation of the criticism is not sufficiently sympathetic. But we cannot afford the space to go into it much further. It seems to me that this criticism depends on a confusion between two kinds of mistake. We may call them 'errors of functioning' and 'errors of conclusion.' Errors of functioning are due to some mechanical or electrical fault which causes the machine to behave otherwise than it was designed to do. In philosophical discussions one likes to ignore the possibility of such errors; one is therefore discussing 'abstract machines.' These abstract machines are mathematical fictions rather than physical objects. By definition they are incapable of errors of functioning. In this sense we can truly say that 'machines can never make mistakes.' Errors of conclusion can only arise when some meaning is attached to the output signals from the machine. The machine might, for instance, type out mathematical equations, or sentences in English. When a false proposition is typed we say that the machine has committed an error of conclusion. There is clearly no reason at all for saying that a machine cannot make this kind of mistake. It might do nothing but type out repeatedly 'O = I.' To take a less perverse example, it might have some method for drawing conclusions by scientific induction. We must expect such a method to lead occasionally to erroneous results.

'Stream of Consciousness'
William James, 1890

> American philosopher and psychologist William James
> (1842–1910) is considered the first thinker to use the term
> 'stream of consciousness', which appears in his book *The
> Principles of Psychology*. Here, James debates the validity of
> this and other metaphors.

Consciousness, then, does not appear to itself chopped up in
bits. Such words as 'chain' or 'train' do not describe it fitly as
it presents itself in the first instance. It is nothing jointed; it
flows. A 'river' or a 'stream' are the metaphors by which it is
most naturally described. *In talking of it hereafter, let us call it the
stream of thought, of consciousness, or of subjective life.*

But now there appears, even with the limits of the same
self, and between thoughts all of which alike have this same
sense of belonging together, a kind of jointing and separate-
ness among the parts, of which this statement seems to
take no account. I refer to the breaks that are produced by
sudden *contrasts in the quality* of the successive segments of
the stream of thought. If the words 'chain' and 'train' had no
natural fitness in them, how came such words to be used at
all? Does not a loud explosion rend the consciousness upon
which it abruptly breaks, in twain? Does not every sudden
shock, appearance of a new object, or change in a sensation,
create a real interruption, sensibly felt as such, which cuts the
conscious stream across at the moment at which it appears?
Do not such interruptions smite us every hour of our lives, and
have we the right, in their presence still to call our consciousness a continuous stream?

This objection is based partly on a confusion and partly on
a superficial introspective view.

The confusion is between the thoughts themselves, taken

as subjective facts, and the things of which they are aware. It is natural to make this confusion, but easy to avoid it when once put on one's guard. The things are discrete and discontinuous; they do pass before us in a train or chain, making often explosive appearances and rending each other in twain. But their comings and goings and contrasts no more break the flow of the thought that thinks them than they break the time and the space in which they lie. A silence may be broken by a thunder-clap, and we may be so stunned and confused for a moment by the shock as to give no instant account to ourselves of what has happened. But that very confusion is a mental state, and a state that passes us straight over from the silence to the sound. The transition between the thought of one object and the thought of another is no more a break in the *thought* than a joint in a bamboo is a break in the wood. It is a part of the *consciousness* as much as the joint is a part of the *bamboo*.

The superficial introspective view is the overlooking, even when the things are contrasted with each other most violently, of the large amount of affinity that may still remain between the thoughts by whose means they are cognised. Into the awareness of the thunder itself the awareness of the previous silence creeps and continues; for what we hear when the thunder crashes is not thunder pure, but thunder-breaking-upon-silence-and-contrasting-with-it. Our feeling of the same objective thunder, coming in this way, is quite different from what it would be were the thunder a continuation of previous thunder. The thunder itself we believe to abolish and exclude the silence; but the *feeling* of the thunder is also a feeling of the silence as just gone; and it would be difficult to find in the actual concrete consciousness of man a feeling so limited to the present as not to have an inkling of anything that went before. Here, again, language works against our perception of the truth. We name our thoughts simply, each after its thing, as if each knew its own thing and nothing else. What each really knows is clearly the thing it is named for, with dimly perhaps a thousand other things. It ought to be named after all of them, but it never is.

'The Proper Approach'
Francis Crick, 1988

British scientist Francis Crick (1916–2004) penned these notes a quarter of a century after sharing the Nobel Prize for his research on the molecular structure of DNA. He later commented that his work on consciousness was unable to explain the many disconnected experimental facts.

1 It is useless to ask how consciousness evolved, since all evolution is difficult and we cannot characterise it clearly in ourselves, let alone higher animals.

2 Nevertheless it is reasonable to assume that the mammals and the primates in particular are conscious. Also it is reasonable to assume that *our* consciousness is more highly developed but based on the same process as in lower animals. Thus all arguments about language and communication between individuals are best left to one side.

3 It is probably not worthwhile arguing what consciousness is *for*, since we don't yet know what it is or how it works.

4 Nevertheless the points that might have arisen in 1 to 3 above *may* be useful as *hints* but are not to be used as arguments.

5 The proper approach is to ask:

a) What are the essential features of consciousness and

b) What removal of apparatus and/or mode of functioning is essential for consciousness.

In discussing 5(a) it is not unreasonable to ask about the nature of consciousness in different *states*, such as REM [rapid eye movement] sleep, SW [slow-wave] sleep, under various anaesthetics etc.

6 The only adequate explanation of consciousness *in the long run* is one based on how neurons and sets of neurons behave, because that is the only satisfactory way to *test* a theory of consciousness.

7 It is a waste of time, at this stage, to ask exactly how one will eventually 'prove' a theory of consciousness.

The Hippocampus
Camillo Golgi, 1903

Italian physician and scientist Camillo Golgi (1843–1926) pioneered a method for staining tissue that revealed individual neurons for the first time. This is a section from Golgi's drawing of the hippocampus.

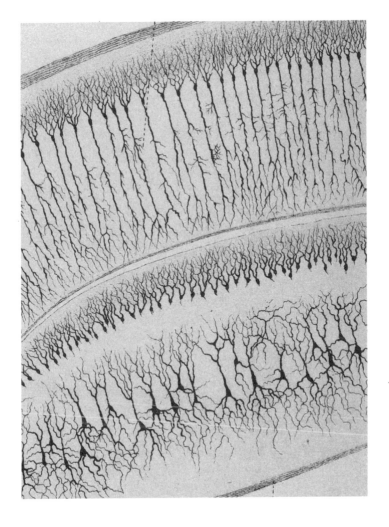

Astrocytes
Santiago Ramón y Cajal, *c.*1904

Spanish scientist Santiago Ramón y Cajal (1852–1934) employed Camillo Golgi's staining techniques, but drew different conclusions about what he observed. These star-like drawings depict the feathery brain cells of a two-month-old child.

Golgi's Door
Katherine Sherwood, 2007

The title of this mixed media artwork by American artist
Katherine Sherwood (b. 1952) alludes to Camillo Golgi's
staining technique, which opened up our understanding
of the nervous system.

The Psychological Working of Colour
Wassily Kandinsky, 1910

> Russian painter Wassily Kandinsky (1866–1944) is thought
> to have seen moving coloured shapes when he listened to
> music. He shared his own theory about synaesthesia, or the
> triggering of one sense by another, in his book *The Art of
> Spiritual Harmony*.

To let the eye stray over a palette, splashed with many colours,
produces a dual result. In the first place one receives a *purely
physical impression*, one of pleasure and contentment at the
varied and beautiful colours. The eye is either warmed or else
soothed and cooled. But these physical sensations can only
be of short duration. They are merely superficial and leave no
lasting impression, for the soul is unaffected. But although the
effect of the colours is forgotten when the eye is turned away,
the superficial impression of varied colour may be the starting
point of a whole chain of related sensations.

On the average man only the impressions caused by very
familiar objects, will be purely superficial. A first encounter
with any new phenomenon exercises immediately an impression on the soul. This is the experience of the child discovering
the world, to whom every object is new. He sees a light, wishes
to take hold of it, burns his finger and feels henceforward
a proper respect for flame. But later he learns that light has
a friendly as well as an unfriendly side, that it drives away
the darkness, makes the day longer, is essential to warmth,
cooking, play-acting. From the mass of these discoveries is
composed a knowledge of light, which is indelibly fixed in
his mind. The strong, intensive interest disappears and the
various properties of flame are balanced against each other.
In this way the whole world becomes gradually disenchanted.
It is realised that trees give shade, that horses run fast and

motor-cars still faster, that dogs bite, that the figure seen in a mirror is not a real human being.

As the man develops, the circle of these experiences caused by different beings and objects, grows ever wider. They acquire an inner meaning and eventually a spiritual harmony. It is the same with colour, which makes only a momentary and superficial impression on a soul but slightly developed in sensitiveness. But even this superficial impression varies in quality. The eye is strongly attracted by light, clear colours, and still more strongly attracted by those colours which are warm as well as clear; vermilion has the charm of flame, which has always attracted human beings. Keen lemon-yellow hurts the eye in time as a prolonged and shrill trumpet-note the ear, and the gazer turns away to seek relief in blue or green.

But to a more sensitive soul the effect of colours is deeper and intensely moving. And so we come to the second main result of looking at colours: *their psychic effect*. They produce a corresponding spiritual vibration, and it is only as a step towards this spiritual vibration that the elementary physical impression is of importance.

Whether the psychic effect of colour is a direct one, as these last few lines imply, or whether it is the outcome of association, is perhaps open to question. The soul being one with the body, the former may well experience a psychic shock, caused by association acting on the latter. For example, red may cause a sensation analogous to that caused by flame, because red is the colour of flame. A warm red will prove exciting, another shade of red will cause pain or disgust through association with running blood. In these cases colour awakens a corresponding physical sensation, which undoubtedly works upon the soul.

If this were always the case, it would be easy to define by association the effects of colour upon other senses than that of sight. One might say that keen yellow looks sour, because it recalls the taste of a lemon.

But such definitions are not universally possible. There are many examples of colour working which refuse to be so classified. A Dresden doctor relates of one of his patients, whom he designates as an 'exceptionally sensitive person,' that he could not eat a certain sauce without tasting 'blue,' i.e. without experiencing a feeling of seeing a blue colour. It would be possible to suggest, by way of explanation of this, that in highly sensitive people, the way to the soul is so direct and the soul itself so impressionable, that any impression of taste communicates itself immediately to the soul, and thence to the other organs of sense (in this case, the eyes). This would imply an echo or reverberation, such as occurs sometimes in musical instruments which, without being touched, sound in harmony with some other instrument struck at the moment.

But not only with taste has sight been known to work in harmony. Many colours have been described as rough or sticky, others as smooth and uniform, so that one feels inclined to stroke them (e.g., dark ultramarine, chromic oxide green, and rose madder). Equally the distinction between warm and cold colours belongs to this connection. Some colours appear soft (rose madder), others hard (cobalt green, blue-green oxide), so that even fresh from the tube they seem to be dry.

The expression 'scented colours' is frequently met with. And finally the sound of colours is so definite that it would be hard to find anyone who would try to express bright yellow in the bass notes, or dark lake in the treble. The explanation by association will not suffice us in many, and the most important, cases. Those who have heard of chromotherapy will know that coloured light can exercise very definite influences on the whole body. Attempts have been made with different colours in the treatment of various nervous ailments. They have shown that red light stimulates and excites the heart, while blue light can cause temporary paralysis. But when the experiments come to be tried on animals and even plants, the association theory falls to the ground. So one is bound to admit that the question is at present unexplored, but that colour can exercise enormous influence over the body as a physical organism.

No more sufficient, in the psychic sphere, is the theory of association. Generally speaking, colour is a power which directly influences the soul. Colour is the keyboard, the eyes are the hammers, the soul is the piano with many strings. The artist is the hand which plays, touching one key or another, to cause vibrations in the soul.

It is evident therefore that colour harmony must rest only on a corresponding vibration in the human soul; and this is one of the guiding principles of the inner need.

'A Bed Filled with Bread Crumbs'
H L Gold, 1953

In Canadian-born science-fiction writer H L Gold's (1914–1996) short story *The Man with English* Edgar Stone wakes up in hospital with a head injury. His accident appears to have altered how his brain interprets information received from the senses.

"God damn it!" Stone yelled. "You could at least turn on the lights."

"There, there, Edgar. Everything's fine, just fine."

It was his wife's voice and the tone was so uncommonly soft and soothing that it scared him into a panic.

"What's wrong with me?" he asked piteously. "Am I blind?"

"How many fingers am I holding up?" a man wanted to know.

Stone was peering into the blackness. All he could see before his eyes was a vague blot against a darker blot.

"None," he bleated. "Who are you?"

"Dr Rankin. That was a nasty fall you had, Mr Stone – concussion of course, and a splinter of bone driven into the brain. I had to operate to remove it."

"Then you cut out a nerve!" Stone said. "You did something to my eyes!"

The doctor's voice sounded puzzled. "There doesn't seem to be anything wrong with them. I'll take a look, though, and see."

"You'll be all right, dear," Mrs Stone said reassuringly, but she didn't sound as if she believed it.

"Sure you will, Pop," said Arnold.

"Is that young stinker here?" Stone demanded. "He's the cause of all this!"

"Temper, temper," the doctor said. "Accidents happen."

Stone heard him lower the venetian blinds. As if they had been a switch, light sprang up and everything in the hospital became brightly visible.

"Well!" said Stone. "That's more like it. It's night and you're trying to save electricity, hey?"

"It's broad daylight, Edgar dear," his wife protested. "All Dr Rankin did was lower the blinds and – "

"Please," the doctor said. "If you don't mind, I'd rather take care of any explanations that have to be made."

He came at Stone with an ophthalmoscope. When he flashed it into Stone's eyes, everything went black and Stone let him know it vociferously.

"Black?" Dr Rankin repeated blankly. "Are you positive? Not a sudden glare?"

"Black," insisted Stone. "And what's the idea of putting me in a bed filled with bread crumbs?"

"It was freshly made – "

"Crumbs. You heard me. And the pillow has rocks in it."

"What else is bothering you?" asked the doctor worriedly.

"It's freezing in here." Stone felt the terror rise in him again. "It was summer when I fell off the ladder. Don't tell me I've been unconscious clear through till winter!"

"No, Pop," said Arnold. "That was yesterday – "

"I'll take care of this," Dr Rankin said firmly. "I'm afraid you and your son will have to leave, Mrs Stone. I have to do a few tests on your husband."

"Will he be all right?" she appealed.

"Of course, of course," he said inattentively, peering with a frown at the shivering patient. "Shock, you know," he added vaguely.

"Gosh, Pop," said Arnold. "I'm sorry this happened. I got the driveway all cleaned up."

"And we'll take care of the store till you're better," Mrs Stone promised.

"Don't you dare!" yelled Stone. "You'll put me out of business!"

The doctor hastily shut the door on them and came back to the bed. Stone was clutching the light summer blanket around himself. He felt colder than he'd ever been in his life.

"Can't you get me more blankets?" he begged. "You don't want me to die of pneumonia, do you?"

Dr Rankin opened the blinds and asked, "What's this like?"

"Night," chattered Stone. "A new idea to save electricity – hooking up the blinds to the light switch?"

The doctor closed the blinds and sat down beside the bed. He was sweating as he reached for the signal button and pressed it. A nurse came in, blinking in their direction.

"Why don't you turn on the light?" she asked.

"Huh?" said Stone. "They are."

"Nurse, I'm Dr Rankin. Get me a piece of sandpaper, some cotton swabs, an ice cube and Mr Stone's lunch."

"Is there anything he shouldn't eat?"

"That's what I want to find out. Hurry, please."

"And some blankets," Stone put in, shaking with the chill.

"Blankets, Doctor?" she asked, startled.

"Half a dozen will do," he said. "I think."

It took her ten minutes to return with all the items. Stone wanted them to keep adding blankets until all seven were on him. He still felt cold.

"Maybe some hot coffee?" he suggested.

The doctor nodded and the nurse poured a cup, added the spoon and a half of sugar he requested, and he took a mouthful. He sprayed it out violently.

"Ice cold!" he yelped. "And who put salt in it?"

"Salt?" She fumbled around on the tray. "It's so dark here –"

"I'll attend to it," Dr Rankin said hurriedly. "Thank you."

She walked cautiously to the door and went out.

"Try this," said the doctor, after filling another cup.

"Well, that's better!" Stone exclaimed. "Damned practical joker. They shouldn't be allowed to work in hospitals."

"And now, if you don't mind," said the doctor, "I'd like to try several tests."

Stone was still angry at the trick played on him, but he cooperated willingly.

Dr Rankin finally sagged back in his chair. The sweat ran down his face and into his collar, and his expression was so dazed that Stone was alarmed.

"What's wrong, Doctor? Am I going to – going to – "

"No, no. It's not that. No danger. At least, I don't believe there is. But I can't even be sure of that any more."

"You can't be sure if I'll live or die?"

"Look." Dr Rankin grimly pulled the chair closer. "It's broad daylight and yet you can't see until I darken the room. The coffee was hot and sweet, but it was cold and salty to you, so I added an ice cube and a spoonful of salt and it tasted fine, you said. This is one of the hottest days on record and you're freezing. You told me the sandpaper felt smooth and satiny, then yelled that somebody had put pins in the cotton swabs, when there weren't any, of course. I've tried you out with different colours around the room and you saw violet when you should have seen yellow, green for red, orange for blue, and so on. Now do you understand?"

"No," said Stone frightenedly. "What's wrong?"

"All I can do is guess. I had to remove that sliver of bone from your brain. It apparently shorted your sensory nerves."

"And what happened?"

"Every one of your senses has been reversed. You feel cold for heat, heat for cold, smooth for rough, rough for smooth, sour for sweet, sweet for sour, and so forth. And you see colours backward."

Stone sat up. "Murderer! Thief! You've ruined me!"

The doctor sprang for a hypodermic and sedative. Just in time, he changed his mind and took a bottle of stimulant instead. It worked fine, though injecting it into his screaming, thrashing patient took more strength than he'd known he owned. Stone fell asleep immediately.

There were nine blankets on Stone and he had a bag of cement for a pillow when he had his lawyer, Manny Lubin, in to hear the charges he wanted brought against Dr Rankin. The doctor was there to defend himself. Mrs Stone was present in spite of her husband's objections – "She always takes everybody's side against me," he explained in a roar.

"I'll be honest with you, Mr Lubin," the doctor said, after Stone had finished on a note of shrill fascination. "I've hunted for cases like this in medical history and this is the first one ever to be reported. Except," he amended quickly, "that I haven't reported it yet. I'm hoping it reverses itself. That sometimes happens, you know."

"And what am I supposed to do in the meantime?" raged Stone. "I'll have to go out wearing an overcoat in the summer and shorts in the winter – people will think I'm a maniac. And they'll be sure of it because I'll have to keep the store closed during the day and open at night – I can't see except in the dark. And matching materials! I can't stand the feel of smooth cloth and I see colours backwards!" He glared at the doctor before turning back to Lubin. "How would you like to have to put sugar on your food and salt in your coffee?"

"But we'll work it out, Edgar dear," his wife soothed. "Arnold and I can take care of the store. You always wanted him to come into the business, so that ought to please you – "

"As long as I'm there to watch him!"

"And Dr Rankin said maybe things will straighten out."

"What about that, Doctor?" asked Lubin. "What are the chances?"

Dr Rankin looked uncomfortable. "I don't know. This has never happened before. All we can do is hope."

"Hope, nothing!" Stone stormed. "I want to sue him. He had no right to go meddling around and turn me upside down. Any jury would give me a quarter of a million!"

"I'm no millionaire, Mr Stone," said the doctor.

"But the hospital has money. We'll sue him and the trustees."

There was a pause while the attorney thought. "I'm afraid we wouldn't have a case, Mr Stone." He went on more rapidly as Stone set up, shivering, to argue loudly. "It was an emergency operation. Any surgeon would have had to operate. Am I right, Dr Rankin?"

The doctor explained what would have happened if he had not removed the pressure on the brain, resulting from the concussion, and the danger that the bone splinter, if not extracted, might have gone on travelling and caused possible paralysis or death.

"That would be better than this," said Stone.

"But medical ethics couldn't allow him to let you die,"

Lubin objected. "He was doing his duty. That's point one."

"Mr Lubin is absolutely right, Edgar," said Mrs Stone.

"There, you see?" screamed her husband. "Everybody's right but me! Will you get her out of here before I have a stroke?"

"Her interests are also involved," Lubin pointed out. "Point two is that the emergency came first, the after-effects couldn't be known or considered."

Dr Rankin brightened. "Any operation involves risk, even the excising of a corn. I had to take those risks."

"You had to take them?" Stone scoffed. "All right, what are you leading up to, Lubin?"

"We'd lose," said the attorney.

Stone subsided, but only for a moment. "So we'll lose. But if we sue, the publicity would ruin him. I want to sue!"

"For what, Edgar dear?" his wife persisted. "We'll have a hard enough time managing. Why throw good money after bad?"

"Why didn't I marry a woman who'd take my side, even when I'm wrong?" moaned Stone. "Revenge, that's what. And he won't be able to practice, so he'll have time to find out if there's a cure... and at no charge, either! I won't pay him another cent!"

The doctor stood up eagerly. "But I'm willing to see what can be done right now. And it wouldn't cost you anything, naturally."

"What do you mean?" Stone challenged suspiciously.

"If I were to perform another operation, I'll be able to see which nerves were involved. There's no need to go into the technical side right now, but it is possible to connect nerves. Of course, there are a good many, which complicates matters, especially since the splinter went through several layers – "

Lubin pointed a lawyer's impaling finger at him. "Are you offering to attempt to correct the injury – gratis?"

"Certainly. I mean to say, I'll do my absolute best. But keep in mind, please, that there is no medical precedent."

The attorney, however, was already questioning Stone and his wife. "In view of the fact that we have no legal grounds whatever for suit, does this offer of settlement satisfy your claim against him?"

"Oh, yes!" Mrs Stone cried.

Her husband hesitated for a while, clearly tempted to take the opposite position out of habit. "I guess so," he reluctantly agreed.

"Well, then it's in your hands, Doctor," said Lubin.

Dr Rankin buzzed excitedly for the nurse. "I'll have him prepared for surgery right away."

"It better work this time," warned Stone, clutching a handful of ice cubes to warm his fingers.

Stone came to foggily. He didn't know it, but he had given the anaesthetist a bewildering problem, which finally had been solved by using fumes of aromatic spirits of ammonia. The four blurred figures around the bed seemed to be leaning precariously toward him.

"Pop!" said Arnold. "Look, he's coming out of it! Pop!"

"Speak to me, Edgar dear," Mrs Stone beseeched.

Lubin said, "See how he is, Doctor."

"He's fine," the doctor insisted heartily, his usual bedside manner evidently having returned. "He must be – the blinds are open and he's not complaining that it's dark or that he's cold." He leaned over the bed. "How are you feeling, Mr Stone?"

It took a minute or two for Stone to move his swollen tongue to answer. He wrinkled his nose in disgust.

"What smells purple?" he demanded.

'Won't She Be Cross?'
Morton Prince, 1906

> American physician Morton Prince's (1854–1929) *The Dissociation of a Personality* was the first book-length account of multiple personalities. The work describes the experiences of 23-year-old Clara Fowler (also known as Christine Beauchamp), who visited Prince complaining of headaches and sleeplessness. Under hypnosis Prince unearthed Fowler's additional states of consciousness, including the childlike Chris.

The difference between the ideals of Miss Beauchamp and her subconscious self offered a constant and entertaining study. One of Miss Beauchamp's prominent characteristics is a sense of responsibility and duty. Amusement plays no part in her conception of life, owing to certain circumstances of her environment. However much one might from a moral point of view admire this characteristic, there was a delightful attractiveness in Chris's absolute disregard of responsibility; she was a child of nature. Though it was not until much later in her career that she had an opportunity to put her own ideas into practice, and to please her own tastes (which she did with a vengeance), she early let her sentiments be known. It was contempt for Miss Beauchamp's ideals which led her to try to give the impression of mental superiority. She had, as we shall see, a certain plausible excuse for this, in that, as a subconscious personality, she *observed things when Miss Beauchamp was absorbed in thought, which the latter did not observe, and remembered much that had been forgotten or never known by her.* When I say that 'as a subconscious personality' she did this I am stating an interpretation of the phenomena which were later observed rather than the actual facts themselves. The facts were that Chris remembered and described having seen and heard much of which Miss Beauchamp was ignorant; such as the face of a passer-by or sounds in the street. This could be experimentally demonstrated. The now generally accepted interpretation of such phenomena is subconscious perception, and there seems to be no way of interpreting the perception which Chris remembered excepting in this way, but it is well to bear in mind that it is an interpretation, otherwise there is danger of statements of fact becoming too broad. In this sense she also could subconsciously interfere with and influence Miss Beauchamp's actions, as when she made her fling down the book and diverted her thoughts to prevent her from reading. Chris thought this was quite sufficient to constitute mental superiority. To draw her out I used to insist that she did not know as much about the psychology of Miss Beauchamp's mind as she asserted. This would annoy her and put her on her mettle to prove her claims. On the first occasion when so taunted she replied peevishly, "You would be more sensible to be friends with me than to say I don't know things when I do," and this I found to be the case. Most of Chris's peculiarities of conduct came from her thoroughly childlike character. Her point of view and knowledge of the world being those of a very young girl, she loved to be thought wicked, though her ideas of wickedness were youthful. She pretended to like French novels, though she could not read French and knew nothing about the literature.

In the course of the interview of May 1, reported in the last chapter, Chris remarked that she smelled the odour of a cigarette which I had been smoking. I offered her one. Delighted at the idea, she accepted, but smoked the cigarette very clumsily. The fact that smoking is something absolutely repugnant to Miss Beauchamp's tastes added to Chris's enjoyment. Her manner was that of a child in mischief.

"Won't she be cross?" she laughed.

"Why?"

"She is not in the habit of smoking cigarettes. *I* shall smoke though."

Miss Beauchamp, when awakened, entirely ignorant of what she had been doing, complained of a bitter taste in her mouth, but could not identify it, and I did not enlighten her. At the next interview I remarked to Chris, "Wasn't it funny to see Miss Beauchamp when she tasted the tobacco in her mouth, and did not know what it was?"

Chris laughed and thought it a great joke. "Yes, she thought you had been putting quinine in her mouth, but did not dare ask you." This remark, later verified by Miss Beauchamp, was one of many which showed Chris had knowledge of Miss Beauchamp's thoughts.

'The Brute that Slept within Me'
Robert Louis Stevenson, 1886

> In Robert Louis Stevenson's (1850–1894) famous novella Henry Jekyll develops a drug that enables him to dissociate two personalities at will. These final passages document Jekyll's efforts to control the increasingly dominant Edward Hyde.

A change had come over me. It was no longer the fear of the gallows, it was the horror of being Hyde that racked me. I received Lanyon's condemnation partly in a dream; it was partly in a dream that I came home to my own house and got into bed. I slept after the prostration of the day, with a stringent and profound slumber which not even the nightmares that wrung me could avail to break. I awoke in the morning shaken, weakened, but refreshed. I still hated and feared the thought of the brute that slept within me, and I had not of course forgotten the appalling dangers of the day before; but

I was once more at home, in my own house and close to my drugs; and gratitude for my escape shone so strong in my soul that it almost rivalled the brightness of hope.

I was stepping leisurely across the court after breakfast, drinking the chill of the air with pleasure, when I was seized again with those indescribable sensations that heralded the change; and I had but the time to gain the shelter of my cabinet, before I was once again raging and freezing with the passions of Hyde. It took on this occasion a double dose to recall me to myself; and alas! Six hours after, as I sat looking sadly in the fire, the pangs returned, and the drug had to be re-administered. In short, from that day forth it seemed only by a great effort as of gymnastics, and only under the immediate stimulation of the drug, that I was able to wear the countenance of Jekyll. At all hours of the day and night, I would be taken with the premonitory shudder; above all, if I slept, or even dozed for a moment in my chair, it was always as Hyde that I awakened. Under the strain of this continually-impending doom and by the sleeplessness to which I now condemned myself, ay, even beyond what I had thought possible to man, I became, in my own person, a creature eaten up and emptied by fever, languidly weak both in body and mind, and solely occupied by one thought: the horror of my other self. But when I slept, or when the virtue of the medicine wore off, I would leap almost without transition (for the pangs of transformation grew daily less marked) into the possession of a fancy brimming with images of terror, a soul boiling with causeless hatreds, and a body that seemed not strong enough to contain the raging energies of life. The powers of Hyde seemed to have grown with the sickliness of Jekyll. And certainly the hate that now divided them was equal on each side. With Jekyll, it was a thing of vital instinct. He had now seen the full deformity of that creature that shared with him some of the phenomena of consciousness, and was co-heir with him to death: and beyond these links of community, which in themselves made the most poignant part of his distress, he thought of Hyde, for all his energy of life, as of something not only hellish but inorganic. This was the shocking thing; that the slime of the pit seemed to utter cries and voices; that the amorphous dust gesticulated and sinned; that what was dead, and had no shape, should usurp the offices of life. And this again, that that insurgent horror was knit to him closer than a wife, closer than an eye; lay caged in his flesh, where he heard it mutter and felt it struggle to be born; and at every hour of weakness, and in the confidence of slumber, prevailed against him and deposed him out of life. The hatred of Hyde for Jekyll, was of a different order. His terror of the gallows drove him continually to commit temporary suicide, and return to his subordinate station of a part instead of a person; but he loathed the necessity, he loathed the despondency into which Jekyll was now fallen, and he resented the dislike with which he was himself regarded. Hence the ape-like tricks that he would play me, scrawling in my own hand blasphemies on the pages of my books, burning the letters and destroying the portrait of my father; and indeed, had it not been for his fear of death, he would long ago have ruined himself in order to involve me in the ruin. But his love of life is wonderful; I go further: I, who sicken and freeze at the mere thought of him, when I recall the abjection and passion of this attachment, and when I know how he fears my power to cut him off by suicide, I find it in my heart to pity him.

It is useless, and the time awfully fails me, to prolong this description; no one has ever suffered such torments, let that suffice; and yet even to these, habit brought – no, not allevi- ation – but a certain callousness of soul, a certain acquiescence of despair; and my punishment might have gone on for years, but for the last calamity which has now fallen, and which has finally severed me from my own face and nature. My provision of the salt, which had never been renewed since the date of the first experiment, began to run low. I sent out for a fresh supply, and mixed the draught; the ebullition followed, and the first change of colour, not the second; I drank it and it was without efficiency. You will learn from Poole how I have had London ransacked; it was in vain; and I am now persuaded that my first supply was impure, and that it was that unknown impurity which lent efficacy to the draught.

About a week has passed, and I am now finishing this statement under the influence of the last of the old powders. This, then, is the last time, short of a miracle, that Henry Jekyll can think his own thoughts or see his own face (now how sadly altered!) in the glass. Nor must I delay too long to bring my writing to an end; for if my narrative has hitherto escaped destruction, it has been by a combination of great prudence and great good luck. Should the throes of change take me in the act of writing it, Hyde will tear it in pieces; but if some time shall have elapsed after I have laid it by, his wonderful selfishness and circumscription to the moment will probably save it once again from the action of his ape-like spite. And indeed the doom that is closing on us both, has already changed and crushed him. Half an hour from now, when I shall again and for ever reindue that hated personality, I know how I shall sit shuddering and weeping in my chair, or continue, with the most strained and fear-struck ecstasy of listening, to pace up and down this room (my last earthly refuge) and give ear to every sound of menace. Will Hyde die upon the scaffold? or will he find courage to release himself at the last moment? God knows; I am careless; this is my true hour of death, and what is to follow concerns another than myself. Here then, as I lay down the pen and proceed to seal up my confession, I bring the life of that unhappy Henry Jekyll to an end.

2: Sleep | Awake

Deep sleep | *Waking* | Dreams | *Dream interpretation* | Jungian analysis | *Visions* | Fear of sleep | *Hallucinations* | Nightmare | *Incubus* | Recurring nightmare | *Sleep paralysis* | Kanashibari | *Daydreaming* | Lucid dreaming | *Dream diaries* | Mesmerism | *Trance* | Animal magnetism | *Sleepwalking*

'The Hour of Deep Sleep'
Charles Sherrington, 1942

> Early in his career English physiologist and Nobel Laureate
> Charles Sherrington (1857–1952) was influenced by the
> work of Santiago Ramón y Cajal. In *Man on His Nature*
> Sherrington explores the brain and its work, including the
> nature of sleep.

Suppose we choose the hour of deep sleep. Then only in some
sparse and out of the way places are nodes flashing and trains
of light-points running. Such places indicate local activity still
in progress. At one such place we can watch the behaviour of
a group of lights perhaps a myriad strong. They are pursuing
a mystic and recurrent manoeuvre as if of some incantational
dance. They are superintending the beating of the heart and
the state of the arteries so that while we sleep the circulation
of the blood is what it should be. The great knotted headpiece
of the whole sleeping system lies for the most part dark, and
quite especially so the roof-brain. Occasionally at places in it
lighted points flash or move but soon subside. Such lighted
points and moving trains of lights are mainly far in the
outskirts, and wink slowly and travel slowly. At intervals even
a gush of sparks wells up and sends a train down the spinal
cord, only to fail to arouse it. Where however the stalk joins the
headpiece, there goes forward in a limited field a remarkable
display. A dense constellation of some thousands of nodal
points bursts out every few seconds into a short phase of
rhythmical flashing. At first a few lights, then more, increasing
in rate and number with a deliberate crescendo to a climax,
then to decline and die away. After due pause the efflores-
cence is repeated. With each such rhythmic outburst goes a
discharge of trains of travelling lights along the stalk and out
of it altogether into a number of nerve-branches. What is this

doing? It manages the taking of our breath the while we sleep.

Should we continue to watch the scheme we should observe after a time an impressive change which suddenly accrues. In the great head-end which has been mostly darkness spring up myriads of twinkling stationary lights and myriads of trains of moving lights of many different directions. It is as though activity from one of those local places which continued restless in the darkened main-mass suddenly spread far and wide and invaded all. The great topmost sheet of the mass, that where hardly a light had twinkled or moved, becomes now a sparkling field of rhythmic flashing points with trains of travelling sparks hurrying hither and thither. The brain is waking and with it the mind is returning. It is as if the Milky Way entered upon some cosmic dance. Swiftly the head-mass becomes an enchanted loom where millions of flashing shuttles weave a dissolving pattern, always a meaningful pattern though never an abiding one; a shifting harmony of sub-patterns. Now as the waking body rouses, sub-patterns of this great harmony of activity stretch down the unlit tracks of the stalk-piece of the scheme. Strings of flashing and travelling sparks engage the lengths of it. This means that the body is up and rises to meet the waking day.

Dissolving pattern after dissolving pattern will, the long day through, without remission melt into and succeed each other in this scheme by which for the moment we figure the brain and spinal cord. Especially, and with complexity incredible, in that part which we were thinking of, the roof-brain. Only after day is done will it quiet down, lapse half-way to extinction, and fall again asleep. Then at last, so far at least as the roof-brain, motor acts cease. The brain is released from the waking day and marshals its factors for its motor acts no more.

The Dream of a Ridiculous Man
Fyodor Dostoyevsky, 1877

> The narrator of Russian novelist Fyodor Dostoyevsky's
> (1821–1881) short story describes being unable to sleep
> through the night for a year. Each evening he sits in an
> armchair, sitting but not thinking. This excerpt recalls the
> night he resolved to kill himself.

Dreams, as we all know, are very queer things: some parts
are presented with appalling vividness, with details worked
up with the elaborate finish of jewellery, while others one
gallops through, as it were, without noticing them at all, as, for
instance, through space and time. Dreams seem to be spurred
on not by reason but by desire, not by the head but by the
heart, and yet what complicated tricks my reason has played
sometimes in dreams, what utterly incomprehensible things
happen to it! My brother died five years ago, for instance. I
sometimes dream of him; he takes part in my affairs, we are
very much interested, and yet all through my dream I quite
know and remember that my brother is dead and buried. How
is it that I am not surprised that, though he is dead, he is here
beside me and working with me? Why is it that my reason
fully accepts it? But enough. I will begin about my dream.
Yes, I dreamed a dream, my dream of the third of November.
They tease me now, telling me it was only a dream. But does
it matter whether it was a dream or reality, if the dream made
known to me the truth? If once one has recognised the truth
and seen it, you know that it is the truth and that there is no
other and there cannot be, whether you are asleep or awake.
Let it be a dream, so be it, but that real life of which you make
so much I had meant to extinguish by suicide, and my dream,
my dream – oh, it revealed to me a different life, renewed, grand
and full of power!

'The Dream'
Unknown artist, 1970s

This dream drawing was produced by a patient undergoing treatment with British psychiatrist Dr Alan McGlashan (1898–1997), a well-known Jungian analyst. In his book *The Savage and Beautiful Country* McGlashan describes dreams as gateways to an ambiguous, dangerous and phantasmal world.

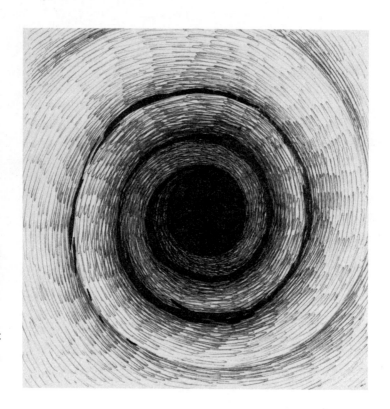

Recollections of Dreamland
James Clerk Maxwell, 1856

Scottish physicist James Clerk Maxwell (1831–1879) is
thought to have written these verses, exploring the power
of dreams to bring the past to mind, a few months after
the death of his father.

Rouse ye! torpid daylight-dreamers, cast your carking
cares away!
As calm air to troubled water, so my night is to your day;
All the dreary day you labour, groping after common
sense,
And your eyes ye will not open on the night's
magnificence.
Ye would scoff were I to tell you how a guiding radiance
gleams
On the outer world of action from my inner world
of dreams.

When, with mind released from study, late I lay
me down to sleep,
From the midst of facts and figures, into boundless
space I leap;
For the inner world grows wider as the outer
disappears,
And the soul, retiring inward, finds itself beyond
the spheres.
Then, to this unbroken sameness, some fantastic
dream succeeds,
Vague emotions rise and ripen into thoughts and
words and deeds.
Old impressions, long forgotten, range themselves

in Time and Space,
Till I recollect the features of some once familiar place.
Then from valley into valley in my dreaming course
    I roam,
Till the wanderings of my fancy end, where they began,
    at home.
Calm it lies in morning twilight, while each streamlet
    far and wide
Still retains its hazy mantle, borrowed from the
    mountain's side;
Every knoll is now an island, every wooded bank a shore,
To the lake of quiet vapour that has spread the
    valley o'er.
Sheep are couched on every hillock, waiting till the
    morning dawns,
Hares are on their early rambles, limping o'er the
    dewy lawns.
All within the house is silent, darkened all the chambers
    seem,
As with noiseless step I enter, gliding onwards in
    my dream.

'The Dream'
Unknown artist, 1970s

This patient's illustration of a dream is full of symbols, providing rich opportunities for an analyst – in this case Dr Alan McGlashan – to explore the turbulent mind of its creator.

Stripes of Conscience
Brocas, 1816

This illustration, from Irish barrister Thomas Grady's satirical poem 'No. III, or, the Nosegay', was published opposite verses describing the torture of night-time reflections:

'Twas then I witness'd of his soul the pangs,
The stripes of conscience, and of guilt the fangs;
Scar'd by fierce visions from his fevri'sh rest,
He saw ten thousand daggers at his breast...

'A True Portrait of My Nights'
Samuel Taylor Coleridge, 1803

> When Samuel Taylor Coleridge (1772–1834) wrote to fellow
> English poet Robert Southey after the death of his friend's
> young daughter he included the first version of a poem later
> entitled 'The Pains of Sleep'. The nightmares Coleridge
> describes may have been caused, or heightened, by his
> opium use.

I have walked 263 miles in eight days, so I must have strength
somewhere, but my spirits are dreadful, owing entirely to the
horrors of every night – I truly dread to sleep. It is no shadow
with me, but substantial misery foot-thick, that makes me sit
by my bedside of a morning and cry. – I have abandoned all
opiates, except ether be one... And when you see me drink a
glass of spirit-and-water, except by prescription of a physician,
you shall despise me, – but still I cannot get quiet rest.

> When on my bed my limbs I lay,
> It hath not been my use to pray
> With moving lips or bended knees;
> But silently, by slow degrees,
> My spirit I to Love compose,
> In humble trust my eyelids close,
> With reverential resignation,
> No wish conceiv'd, no thought exprest,
> Only a *Sense* of supplication,
> A *Sense* o'er all my soul imprest
> That I am weak, yet not unblest,
> Since round me, in me, everywhere
> Eternal strength and Goodness are! –

But yester-night I pray'd aloud
In anguish and in agony,
Awaking from the fiendish crowd
Of shapes and thoughts that tortur'd me!
Desire with loathing strangely mixt,
On wild or hateful objects fixt.
Sense of revenge, the powerless will,
Still baffled and consuming still;
Sense of intolerable wrong,
And men whom I despis'd made strong!
Vain glorious threats, unmanly vaunting,
Bad men my boasts and fury taunting;
Rage, sensual passion, mad'ning Brawl,
And shame and terror over all!
Deeds to be hid that were not hid,
Which all confus'd I might not know,
Whether I suffer'd or I did:
For all was Horror, Guilt, and Woe,
My own or others still the same,
Life-stifling Fear, soul-stifling Shame!

Thus two nights pass'd: the night's dismay
Sadden'd and stunn'd the boding day.
I fear'd to sleep: Sleep seemed to be
Disease's worst malignity.
The third night, when my own loud scream
Had freed me from the fiendish dream,
O'ercome by sufferings dark and wild,
I wept as I had been a child;
And having thus by Tears subdued
My Trouble to a milder mood,
Such punishments, I thought, were due

> To Natures, deepliest stain'd with Sin;
> Still to be stirring up anew
> The self-created Hell within,
> The Horror of the crimes to view,
> To know and loathe, yet wish to do!
> With such let fiends make mockery –
> But I – Oh, wherefore this *on me?*
> Frail is my soul, yea, strengthless wholly,
> Unequal, restless, melancholy;
> But free from Hate and sensual Folly!
> To live belov'd is all I need,
> And whom I love, I love indeed,
>   And etc., etc., etc., etc.

I do not know how I came to scribble down these verses to you – my heart was aching, my head all confused – but they are, doggerel as they may be, a true portrait of my nights.

Hypnos
H P Lovecraft, 1923

American horror author H P Lovecraft (1890–1937) summarised the plot of *Hypnos* as: "The man who would not sleep – dares not sleep – takes drugs to keep himself awake. Finally falls asleep – and *something* happens." The narrator, a sculptor, courts "terrible and forbidden dreams" with a man he befriended at a railway station.

There was a night when winds from unknown spaces whirled us irresistibly into limitless vacua beyond all thought and entity. Perceptions of the most maddeningly untransmissible sort thronged upon us; perceptions of infinity which at the time convulsed us with joy, yet which are now partly lost to my memory and partly incapable of presentation to others. Viscous obstacles were clawed through in rapid succession, and at length I felt that we had been borne to realms of greater remoteness than any we had previously known.

My friend was vastly in advance as we plunged into this awesome ocean of virgin aether, and I could see the sinister exultation on his floating, luminous, too-youthful memory-face. Suddenly that face became dim and quickly disappeared, and in a brief space I found myself projected against an obstacle which I could not penetrate. It was like the others, yet incalculably denser; a sticky clammy mass, if such terms can be applied to analogous qualities in a non-material sphere.

I had, I felt, been halted by a barrier which my friend and leader had successfully passed. Struggling anew, I came to the end of the drug-dream and opened my physical eyes to the tower studio in whose opposite corner reclined the pallid and still unconscious form of my fellow dreamer, weirdly haggard and wildly beautiful as the moon shed gold-green light on his marble features.

Then, after a short interval, the form in the corner stirred; and may pitying heaven keep from my sight and sound another thing like that which took place before me. I cannot tell you how he shrieked, or what vistas of unvisitable hells gleamed for a second in black eyes crazed with fright. I can only say that I fainted, and did not stir till he himself recovered and shook me in his phrensy for someone to keep away the horror and desolation .

That was the end of our voluntary searchings in the caverns of dream. Awed, shaken, and portentous, my friend who had been beyond the barrier warned me that we must never venture within those realms again. What he had seen, he dared not tell me; but he said from his wisdom that we must sleep as little as possible, even if drugs were necessary to keep us awake. That he was right, I soon learned from the unutterable fear which engulfed me whenever consciousness lapsed.

After each short and inevitable sleep I seemed older, whilst my friend aged with a rapidity almost shocking. It is hideous to see wrinkles form and hair whiten almost before one's eyes. Our mode of life was now totally altered. Heretofore a recluse so far as I know – his true name and origin never having passed his lips – my friend now became frantic in his fear of solitude. At night he would not be alone, nor would the company of a few persons calm him. His sole relief was obtained in revelry of the most general and boisterous sort; so that few assemblies of the young and gay were unknown to us.

Our appearance and age seemed to excite in most cases a ridicule which I keenly resented, but which my friend considered a lesser evil than solitude. Especially was he afraid to be out of doors alone when the stars were shining, and if forced to this condition he would often glance furtively at the sky as if hunted by some monstrous thing therein. He did not always glance at the same place in the sky – it seemed to be a different place at different times. On spring evenings it would be low in the northeast. In the summer it would be nearly overhead. In the autumn it would be in the northwest. In winter it would be in the east, but mostly if in the small hours of morning.

Midwinter evenings seemed least dreadful to him. Only after two years did I connect this fear with anything in particular; but then I began to see that he must be looking at a special spot on the celestial vault whose position at different times corresponded to the direction of his glance – a spot roughly marked by the constellation Corona Borealis.

We now had a studio in London, never separating, but never discussing the days when we had sought to plumb the mysteries of the unreal world. We were aged and weak from our drugs, dissipations, and nervous overstrain, and the thinning hair and beard of my friend had become snow-white. Our freedom from long sleep was surprising, for seldom did we succumb more than an hour or two at a time to the shadow which had now grown so frightful a menace.

Then came one January of fog and rain, when money ran low and drugs were hard to buy. My statues and ivory heads were all sold, and I had no means to purchase new materials, or energy to fashion them even had I possessed them. We suffered terribly, and on a certain night my friend sank into a deep-breathing sleep from which I could not awaken him. I can recall the scene now – the desolate, pitch-black garret studio under the eaves with the rain beating down; the ticking of our lone clock; the fancied ticking of our watches as they rested on the dressing-table; the creaking of some swaying shutter in a remote part of the house; certain distant city noises muffled by fog and space; and, worst of all, the deep, steady, sinister breathing of my friend on the couch – a rhythmical breathing which seemed to measure moments of supernal fear and agony for his spirit as it wandered in spheres forbidden, unimagined, and hideously remote.

The tension of my vigil became oppressive, and a wild train of trivial impressions and associations thronged through my almost unhinged mind. I heard a clock strike somewhere – not ours, for that was not a striking clock – and my morbid fancy found in this a new starting-point for idle wanderings. Clocks – time – space – infinity – and then my fancy reverted to the locale as I reflected that even now, beyond the roof and the fog and the rain and the atmosphere, Corona Borealis was rising in the northeast. Corona Borealis, which my friend had appeared to dread, and whose scintillant semicircle of stars must even now be glowing unseen through the measureless abysses of aether. All at once my feverishly sensitive ears seemed to detect a new and wholly distinct component in the soft medley of drug-magnified sounds – a low and damnably insistent whine from very far away; droning, clamouring, mocking, calling, *from the northeast*.

But it was not that distant whine which robbed me of my faculties and set upon my soul such a seal of fright as may never in life be removed; not that which drew the shrieks and excited the convulsions which caused lodgers and police to break down the door. It was not what I heard, but what I saw; for in that dark, locked, shuttered, and curtained room there appeared from the black northeast corner a shaft of horrible red-gold light – a shaft which bore with it no glow to disperse the darkness, but which streamed only upon the recumbent head of the troubled sleeper, bringing out in hideous duplication the luminous and strangely youthful memory-face as I had known it in dreams of abysmal space and unshackled time, when my friend had pushed behind the barrier to those secret, innermost and forbidden caverns of nightmare.

And as I looked, I beheld the head rise, the black, liquid, and deep-sunken eyes open in terror, and the thin, shadowed lips part as if for a scream too frightful to be uttered. There dwelt in that ghastly and flexible face, as it shone bodiless, luminous, and rejuvenated in the blackness, more of stark, teeming, brain-shattering fear than all the rest of heaven and earth has ever revealed to me.

No word was spoken amidst the distant sound that grew nearer and nearer, but as I followed the memory-face's mad stare along that cursed shaft of light to its source, the source whence also the whining came, I, too, saw for an instant what it saw, and fell with ringing ears in that fit of shrieking epilepsy which brought the lodgers and the police. Never could I tell, try as I might, what it actually was that I saw; nor could the still face tell, for although it must have seen more than I did, it will never speak again. But always I shall guard against the mocking and insatiate Hypnos, lord of sleep, against the night sky, and against the mad ambitions of knowledge and philosophy.

Just what happened is unknown, for not only was my own

mind unseated by the strange and hideous thing, but others were tainted with a forgetfulness which can mean nothing if not madness. They have said, I know not for what reason, that I never had a friend; but that art, philosophy, and insanity had filled all my tragic life. The lodgers and police on that night soothed me, and the doctor administered something to quiet me, nor did anyone see what a nightmare event had taken place. My stricken friend moved them to no pity, but what they found on the couch in the studio made them give me a praise which sickened me, and now a fame which I spurn in despair as I sit for hours, bald, grey-bearded, shrivelled, palsied, drug-crazed, and broken, adoring and praying to the object they found.

For they deny that I sold the last of my statuary, and point with ecstasy at the thing which the shining shaft of light left cold, petrified, and unvocal. It is all that remains of my friend; the friend who led me on to madness and wreckage; and godlike head of such marble as only old Hellas could yield, young with the youth that is outside time, and with beauteous bearded face, curved, smiling lips, Olympian brow, and dense locks waving and poppy-crowned. They say that that haunting memory-face is modelled from my own, as it was at twenty-five; but upon the marble base is carven a single name in the letters of Attica – HYPNOS.

Hypnos
Fred Holland Day, *c.*1896

Hypnos is the Greek god of sleep, the twin brother of Death. This portrait by American photographer Fred Holland Day (1864–1933) depicts Hypnos inhaling the hallucinatory scent of a poppy.

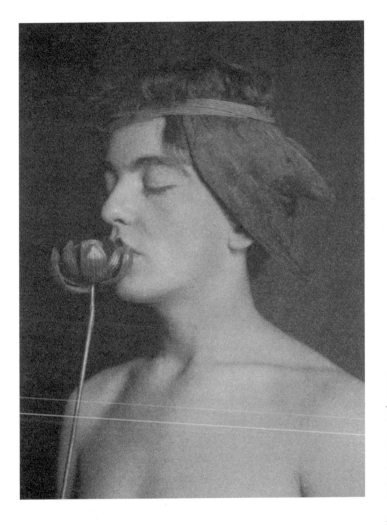

'Oliver Twist Sleeps'
Charles Dickens, 1838

The eponymous hero of Charles Dickens's (1812–1870)
Oliver Twist often appears asleep. Here, Oliver experiences
a disturbing vision while he dozes.

The little room in which he was accustomed to sit when busy
at his books was on the ground-floor, at the back of the house.
It was quite a cottage-room, with a lattice-window, around
which were clusters of jessamine and honeysuckle, that crept
over the casement, and filled the place with their delicious
perfume. It looked into a garden, whence a wicket-gate opened
into a small paddock; all beyond was fine meadow-land and
wood. There was no other dwelling near, in that direction, and
the prospect it commanded was very extensive.

One beautiful evening, when the first shades of twilight
were beginning to settle upon the earth, Oliver sat at this
window, intent upon his books. He had been poring over them
for some time; and as the day had been uncommonly sultry
and he had exerted himself a great deal, it is no disparagement
to the authors, whoever they may have been, to say that gradually and by slow degrees he fell asleep.

There is a kind of sleep that steals upon us sometimes,
which, while it holds the body prisoner, does not free the mind
from a sense of things about it, and enable it to ramble as it
pleases. So far as an overpowering heaviness, a prostration
of strength, and an utter inability to control our thoughts or
power of motion, can be called sleep, this is it; and yet we have
a consciousness of all that is going on about us, and even if we
dream, words which are really spoken, or sounds which really
exist at the moment, accommodate themselves with surprising
readiness to our visions, until reality and imagination become
so strangely blended that it is afterwards almost a matter of

impossibility to separate the two. Nor is this the most striking phenomenon incidental to such a state. It is an ascertained fact, that although our sense of touch and sight be for the time dead, yet our sleeping thoughts and the visionary scenes that pass before us will be influenced and materially influenced, by the *mere silent presence* of some external object which may not have been near us when we closed our eyes, and of whose vicinity we have had no waking consciousness.

Oliver knew perfectly well that he was in his own little room, that his books were lying on the table before him, and that the sweet air was stirring among the creeping plants outside, – and yet he was asleep. Suddenly the scene changed, the air became close and confined, and he thought with a glow of terror that he was in the Jew's house again. There sat the hideous old man, in his accustomed corner pointing at him, and whispering to another man with his face averted who sat beside him.

"Hush, my dear!" he thought he heard the Jew say; "it is him, sure enough. Come away."

"He!" the other man seemed to answer; "could I mistake him, think you? If a crowd of ghosts were to put themselves into his exact shape, and he stood amongst them, there is something that would tell me to point him out. If you buried him fifty feet deep, and took me across his grave, I should know, if there wasn't a mark above it, that he lay buried there. Wither his flesh, I should!"

The man seemed to say this with such dreadful hatred, that Oliver awoke with the fear and started up.

Good God! what was that which sent the blood tingling to his heart, and deprived him of voice or power to move! There – there – at the window – close before him – so close, that he could have almost touched him before he started back – with his eyes peering into the room, and meeting his – there stood the Jew! and beside him, white with rage, or fear, or both, were the scowling features of the very man who had accosted him in the inn-yard.

It was but an instant, a glance, a flash before his eyes, and they were gone. But they had recognised him, and he them, and their look was as firmly impressed upon his memory as if it had been deeply carved in stone, and set before him from his birth. He stood transfixed for a moment, and then, leaping from the window into the garden, called loudly for help.

Etymologies of the Nightmare Experience
Owen Davies, 2003

> British historian Owen Davies (b. 1969) identifies nightmare as a unique human experience "when reality, hallucination, and belief fuse", producing powerful fantasies. This excerpt from a paper published in the journal *Folklore* explores nightmare terminology across different cultures.

The 'mare' element of the English 'nightmare' derives from the same root as the Germanic *mahr* and Old Norse *mara*, a supernatural being, usually female, who lay on people's chests at night, thereby suffocating them. Even if knowledge of the 'mare' has been largely forgotten, she has left her mark in many European languages. In Norway to have the nightmare is to *mareritt*, and we find *nachtmahr* in German, *nachtmerrie* in Dutch, and *cauchemar* in French. The mare concept also forms the basis of Slavic and other central and eastern European terms for nightmare – *zmora* in Polish, *morica* in Croatian, *mòre* in Serbian, *muera* in Czech, *kikimora* in Russian. The presence of the mare in so many languages has understandably led etymologists to assume that it is of Indo-European origin, although there seems no agreement as to its Indo-European meaning. *Móros* ('death'), *mer* ('drive out'), and *mar* ('to pound, bruise, crush') have all been suggested[1].

The sense of pressure or weight is integral to the nightmare both as a concept and as an experience, and so it [is] not surprising that it is also prominent in the linguistics. The first element of French *cauchemar* derives from *caucher* ('to tread on'). The second element of Icelandic *martröd* comes from *troda*, meaning 'to squeeze, press, ride.' The idea of pressure is also present in other terms for the nightmare experience that do not share the *mare* element. In German we find *alpdrücken* ('elf-pressing') and *hexendrücken* ('witch-pressing'). The term for the nightmare in medieval French, *appesart*, Italian *pesuarole*, Spanish *pesadilla*, and Portuguese *pesadela* all derive from the verb *peser*, meaning 'to press down upon'[2]. Latin *incubus* derives from *incubare* ('to lie down upon'). Hungarian *boszorkany-nyomas* means 'witches pressure.' The Estonian word for nightmare, *luupainaja*, means 'the one who presses your bones,' and the Finnish *painajainen* similarly describes 'something weighing upon you.' In Irish, *tromluí* or *tromlaige* likewise derives from the act of weighing or being pressed upon. The same sensation was also expressed in terms of being straddled across the chest and ridden like a horse, as in Norwegian *mareritt*, and English 'witch-ridden' and 'hag-ridden', with dialect variants such as 'hag-rod' and 'hag-rided' in England and Newfoundland.

1 Pócs E. Between the Living and the Dead. Budapest: Central European University Press; 1999.
   Skeat W. The Concise Dictionary of English Etymology. Third edition. Oxford: Clarendon Press; 1888.
2 Lecouteux C. Mara – ephialtes – incubus: le cauchemar chez les peuples germaniques. Études Germaniques 1987;42:1–24.
   Lecouteux C. Les Nains et les Elfes au Moyen Âge. Paris: Imago; 1988.

Nightmare
Thomas Holloway after Henry Fuseli, 1791

When Swiss-born painter Henry Fuseli (1741–1825) exhibited his painting *The Nightmare* at the Royal Academy's annual exhibition in 1782 it caused a sensation. This variation on his original depicts the same demonic imp crouching on a sleeping woman's chest, a composition some interpreted as a physical representation of the nightmare; others viewed it as a shocking symbol of sexual desire.

NIGHTMARE | INCUBUS

'The Will Presides Not'
Erasmus Darwin, 1789

Physician, natural philosopher and poet Erasmus Darwin
(1731–1802) employed Henry Fuseli to illustrate his book
The Botanic Garden, placing these verses by the engraving
opposite. Darwin described incubus as "a painful desire" to
control voluntary motions while asleep.

So on his Nightmare through the evening fog
Flits the squab Fiend o'er fen, and lake, and bog;
Seeks some love-wilder'd Maid with sleep oppress'd,
Alights, and grinning sits upon her breast.
– Such as of late amid the murky sky
Was mark'd by Fuseli's poetic eye;
Whose daring tints, with Shakespear's happiest grace,
Gave to the airy phantom form and place. –
Back o'er her pillow sinks her blushing head,
Her snow-white limbs hang helpless from the bed;
While with quick sighs, and suffocative breath,
Her interrupted heart-pulse swims in death.
– Then shrieks of captur'd towns, and widows' tears,
Pale lovers stretch'd upon their blood-stain'd biers,
The headlong precipice that thwarts her flight,
The trackless desert, the cold starless night,
And stern-eye'd Murderer with his knife behind,
In dread succession agonise her mind.
O'er her fair limbs convulsive tremors fleet,
Start in her hands, and struggle in her feet;
In vain to scream with quivering lips she tries,
And strains in palsy'd lids her tremulous eyes;
In vain she *wills* to run, fly, swim, walk, creep;

The Will presides not in the bower of Sleep.
– On her fair bosom sits the Demon-Ape
Erect, and balances his bloated shape;
Rolls in their marble orbs his Gorgon-eyes,
And drinks with leathern ears her tender cries.

A Child's Nightmare
Robert Graves, 1917

English poet Robert Graves (1895–1985) wrote these verses, describing a hideous childhood dream haunting a wounded soldier, while serving on the Western Front.

Through long nursery nights he stood
By my bed unwearying,
Loomed gigantic, formless, queer,
Purring in my haunted ear
That same hideous nightmare thing,
Talking, as he lapped my blood,
In a voice cruel and flat,
Saying for ever, "Cat!... Cat!... Cat!..."

That one word was all he said,
That one word through all my sleep,
In monotonous mock despair.
Nonsense may be light as air,
But there's Nonsense that can keep
Horror bristling round the head,
When a voice cruel and flat
Says for ever, "Cat!... Cat!... Cat!..."

He had faded, he was gone
Years ago with Nursery Land,
When he leapt on me again
From the clank of a night train,
Overpowered me foot and hand,
Lapped my blood, while on and on
The old voice cruel and flat
Purred for ever, "Cat!... Cat!... Cat!..."

Morphia drowsed, again I lay
In a crater by High Wood:
He was there with straddling legs,
Staring eyes as big as eggs,
Purring as he lapped my blood,
His black bulk darkening the day,
With a voice cruel and flat,
 "Cat!... Cat!... Cat!..." he said, "Cat!... Cat!..."

When I'm shot through heart and head,
And there's no choice but to die,
The last word I'll hear, no doubt,
Won't be "Charge!" or "Bomb them out!"
Nor the stretcher-bearer's cry,
 "Let that body be, he's dead!"
But a voice cruel and flat
Saying for ever, "Cat!... Cat!... Cat!..."

The Counterpane
Herman Melville, 1851

> In Herman Melville's (1819–1891) novel *Moby-Dick* the
> narrator Ishmael recounts an unsettling childhood
> experience. Ishmael's inability to speak or move while
> remaining conscious of his environment is consistent
> with what is now termed 'sleep paralysis'.

Upon waking next morning about daylight, I found
Queequeg's arm thrown over me in the most loving and affec-
tionate manner. You had almost thought I had been his wife.
The counterpane was of patchwork, full of odd little parti-
coloured squares and triangles; and this arm of his tattooed all
over with an interminable Cretan labyrinth of a figure, no two
parts of which were of one precise shade – owing I suppose to
his keeping his arm at sea unmethodically in sun and shade,
his shirt sleeves irregularly rolled up at various times – this
same arm of his, I say, looked for all the world like a strip of
that same patchwork quilt. Indeed, partly lying on it as the arm
did when I first awoke, I could hardly tell it from the quilt, they
so blended their hues together; and it was only by the sense
of weight and pressure that I could tell that Queequeg was
hugging me.

My sensations were strange. Let me try to explain them.
When I was a child, I well remember a somewhat similar
circumstance that befell me; whether it was a reality or a
dream, I never could entirely settle. The circumstance was
this. I had been cutting up some caper or other – I think it was
trying to crawl up the chimney, as I had seen a little sweep do a
few days previous; and my stepmother who, somehow or other,
was all the time whipping me, or sending me to bed supper-
less, – my mother dragged me by the legs out of the chimney
and packed me off to bed, though it was only two o'clock in the

afternoon of the 21st June, the longest day in the year in our hemisphere. I felt dreadfully. But there was no help for it, so up stairs I went to my little room in the third floor, undressed myself as slowly as possible so as to kill time, and with a bitter sigh got between the sheets.

I lay there dismally calculating that sixteen entire hours must elapse before I could hope for a resurrection. Sixteen hours in bed! the small of my back ached to think of it. And it was so light too; the sun shining in at the window, and a great rattling of coaches in the streets, and the sound of gay voices all over the house. I felt worse and worse – at last I got up, dressed and softly going down in my stockinged feet, sought out my stepmother, and suddenly threw myself at her feet, beseeching her as a particular favour to give me a good slippering for my misbehaviour; anything indeed but condemning me to lie abed such an unendurable length of time. But she was the best and most conscientious of stepmothers, and back I had to go to my room. For several hours I lay there broad awake, feeling a great deal worse than I have ever done since, even from the greatest subsequent misfortunes. At last I must have fallen into a troubled nightmare of a doze; and slowly waking from it – half steeped in dreams – I opened my eyes, and the before sun-lit room was now wrapped in outer darkness. Instantly I felt a shock running through all my frame; nothing was to be seen, and nothing was to be heard; but a supernatural hand seemed placed in mine. My arm hung over the counterpane, and the nameless, unimaginable, silent form or phantom, to which the hand belonged, seemed closely seated by my bedside. For what seemed ages piled on ages, I lay there, frozen with the most awful fears, not daring to drag away my hand; yet ever thinking that if I could but stir it one single inch, the horrid spell would be broken. I knew not how this consciousness at last glided away from me; but waking in the morning, I shudderingly remembered it all, and for days and weeks and months afterwards I lost myself in confounding attempts to explain the mystery. Nay, to this very hour, I often puzzle myself with it.

Fudō Myō-ō
Unknown artist, 17th century?

The Buddhist deity Fudō Myō-ō, who carries a chain, is always ready to bind and incapacitate his evil enemies. Praying to Fudō Myō-ō may summon an immobilising '*kanashibari* spell' reminiscent of sleep paralysis.

Sleep
Haruki Murakami, 1992

> Japanese author Haruki Murakami's (b. 1949) short
> story starts with the line "This is my seventeenth straight
> day without sleep", yet the narrator does not suffer
> from insomnia. This extract illustrates the paralysing
> phenomenon known in Japan as *kanashibari*, meaning
> 'binding tightly'.

I remember with perfect clarity that first night I lost the ability
to sleep. I was having a repulsive dream – a dark, slimy dream.
I don't remember what it was about, but I do remember how
it felt: ominous and terrifying. I woke at the climactic moment
– came fully awake with a start, as if something had dragged
me back at the last moment from a fatal turning point. Had
I remained immersed in the dream for another second, I
would have been lost forever. After I awoke, my breath came in
painful gasps for a time. My arms and legs felt paralysed. I lay
there immobilised, listening to my own laboured breathing, as
if I were stretched out full-length on the floor of a huge cavern.

"It was a dream," I told myself, and I waited for my
breathing to calm down. Lying stiff on my back, I felt my heart
working violently, my lungs hurrying the blood to it with big,
slow, bellowslike contractions. I began to wonder what time
it could be. I wanted to look at the clock by my pillow, but
I couldn't turn my head far enough. Just then, I seemed to
catch a glimpse of something at the foot of the bed, something
like a vague, black shadow. I caught my breath. My heart, my
lungs, everything inside me, seemed to freeze in that instant. I
strained to see the black shadow.

The moment I tried to focus on it, the shadow began to
assume a definite shape, as if it had been waiting for me to
notice it. Its outline became distinct, and began to be filled

with substance, and then with details. It was a gaunt old man wearing a skintight black shirt. His hair was grey and short, his cheeks shrunken. He stood at my feet, perfectly still. He said nothing, but his piercing eyes stared at me. They were huge eyes, and I could see the red network of veins in them. The old man's face wore no expression at all. It told me nothing. It was like an opening in the darkness.

This was no longer the dream, I knew. From that I had already awakened. And not just by drifting awake, but by having my eyes ripped open. No, this was no dream. This was reality. And in reality an old man I had never seen before was standing at the foot of my bed. I had to do something – turn on the light, wake my husband, scream. I tried to move. I fought to make my limbs work, but it did no good. I couldn't move a finger. When it became clear to me that I would never be able to move, I was filled with a hopeless terror, a primal fear such as I had never experienced before, like a chill that rises silently from the bottomless well of memory. I tried to scream, but I was incapable of producing a sound, or even moving my tongue. All I could do was look at the old man.

Now I saw that he was holding something – a tall, narrow, rounded thing that shone white. As I stared at this object, wondering what it could be, it began to take on a definite shape, just as the shadow had earlier. It was a pitcher, an old-fashioned porcelain pitcher. After some time, the man raised the pitcher and began pouring water from it onto my feet. I could not feel the water. I could see it and hear it splashing down onto my feet, but I couldn't feel a thing.

The old man went on and on pouring water over my feet. Strange – no matter how much he poured, the pitcher never ran dry. I began to worry that my feet would eventually rot and melt away. Yes, of course they would rot. What else could they do with so much water pouring over them? When it occurred to me that my feet were going to rot and melt away, I couldn't take it any longer.

I closed my eyes and let out a scream so loud it took every ounce of strength I had. But it never left my body. It reverberated soundlessly inside, tearing through me, shutting down my heart. Everything inside my head turned white for a moment as the scream penetrated my every cell. Something inside me died. Something melted away, leaving only a shuddering vacuum. An explosive flash incinerated everything my existence depended on.

When I opened my eyes, the old man was gone. The pitcher was gone. The bedspread was dry, and there was no indication that anything near my feet had been wet. My body, though, was soaked with sweat, a horrifying volume of sweat, more sweat than I ever imagined a human being could produce. And yet, undeniably, it was sweat that had come from me.

I moved one finger. Then another, and another, and the rest. Next, I bent my arms and then my legs. I rotated my feet and bent my knees. Nothing moved quite as it should have, but at least it did move. After carefully checking to see that all my body parts were working. I eased myself into a sitting position. In the dim light filtering in from the streetlamp, I scanned the entire room from corner to corner. The old man was definitely not there.

The clock by my pillow said 12:30. I had been sleeping for only an hour and a half. My husband was sound asleep in his bed. Even his breathing was inaudible. He always sleeps like that, as if all mental activity in him had been obliterated. Almost nothing can wake him.

I got out of bed and went to the bathroom. I threw my sweat-soaked nightgown into the washing machine and took a shower. After putting on a fresh pair of pyjamas, I went to the living room, switched on the floor lamp beside the sofa, and sat there drinking a full glass of brandy. I almost never drink. Not that I have a physical incompatibility with alcohol, as my husband does. In fact, I used to drink quite a lot, but after marrying him I simply stopped. Sometimes when I had trouble sleeping I would take a sip of brandy, but that night I felt I wanted a whole glass to quiet my overwrought nerves.

The only alcohol in the house was a bottle of Rémy Martin we kept in the sideboard. It had been a gift. I don't even remember who gave it to us, it was so long ago. The bottle wore a thin layer of dust. We had no real brandy glasses, so I just poured it into a regular tumbler and sipped it slowly.

I must have been in a trance, I thought. I had never experienced such a thing, but I had heard about trances from a college friend who had been through one. Everything was incredibly clear, she had said. You can't believe it's a dream. "I didn't believe it was a dream when it was happening, and now I still don't believe it was a dream." Which is exactly how I felt. Of course it had to be a dream – a kind of dream that doesn't feel like a dream.

Though the terror was leaving me, the trembling of my body would not stop. It was in my skin, like the circular ripples on water after an earthquake. I could see the slight quivering. The scream had done it. The scream that had never found a voice was still locked up in my body, making it tremble.

I closed my eyes and swallowed another mouthful of brandy. The warmth spread from my throat to my stomach. The sensation felt tremendously *real*.

With a start, I thought of my son. Again my heart began pounding. I hurried from the sofa to his room. He was sound asleep, one hand across his mouth, the other thrust out to the side, looking just as secure and peaceful in sleep as my husband. I straightened his blanket. Whatever it was that had so violently shattered my sleep, it had attacked only me. Neither of them had felt a thing.

Reverie
Robert Macnish, 1830

In what he claimed to be the first complete treatise on the topic, Scottish surgeon Robert Macnish (1802–1837) defined sleep as the "intermediate state between life and death". This extract from *The Philosophy of Sleep* is taken from the chapter on 'Reverie'.

A state of mind somewhat analogous to that which prevails in dreaming, also takes place during reverie. There is the same want of balance in the faculties, which are almost equally ill regulated, and disposed to indulge in similar extravagancies. Reverie proceeds from the inability of the mind to direct itself strongly to any single point. There is a defect in the *attention*, which, instead of being fixed to one, wanders over a thousand subjects, and even on these is feebly and ineffectively directed. We sometimes see this while reading, or, rather, while attempting to read. We get over page after page, but the ideas take no hold whatever upon us: we are, in truth, ignorant of what we peruse, and the mind is either an absolute blank, or vaguely addressed to something else. This feeling every person must have occasionally noticed, in taking out his watch, looking at it, and replacing it without knowing what the hour was. In like manner, he may hear what is said to him, without attaching any meaning to the words, which strike his ear, yet communicate no idea to the sensorium – while he continues to pursue a train of cogitations widely different. That kind of reverie, in which the mind is divested of all ideas, and approximates closely to the state of sleep, I have sometimes experienced while gazing long and intently upon a river. The thoughts seem to glide away one by one, upon the surface of the stream, till the mind is emptied of them altogether – in other words, till the thinking principle of the brain is wholly stripped of its sensorial power. In this state, we still see the glassy volume of the water moving past us, and hear its murmur, but lose all power of reflecting upon these or any other subjects; and either fall asleep, or are aroused by some spontaneous reaction of the mind, or by some appeal to the senses, sufficiently strong to startle us from our reverie.

Reverie is most apt to ensue in the midst of perfect silence; hence in walking alone in the country, where there is no sound to distract our meditations, we frequently get into this state. It is also apt to take place when we are seated, without companions, or books, or amusement of any kind, by the hearth, on a winter evening, especially when the fire is beginning to burn out, when the candles are becoming faint for want of topping, and a dim religious light, like that filling a hermit's cell from his solitary lamp, is diffused over the apartment. This is the situation most favourable for reverie, day-dreams, and all kinds of brown-study, abstraction, ennui and hypochondria.

The Bride of Dreams
Frederik van Eeden, 1913

Dutch psychiatrist Frederik van Eeden (1860–1932), who claimed to experience 352 lucid dreams between 1897 and 1913, described lucid dreaming as a "sphere of ecstasy and great joy" where "consciousness of self is strongest". These passages are taken from Van Eeden's novel *The Bride of Dreams*.

Now it also seems to me that he who dreams is more awake than he who sleeps, and that he who spends a third part of his life in utter unconsciousness better deserves to be called a sleepyhead and dullard, than he for whom the dark nights are also vivid and rich with pulsing life. To me it has always

LUCID DREAMING

seemed a shame to lie like a stone for so many hours, and
to arise from sleep no wiser than when we sank into it. And
after having experienced several times in my early youth that
sleep possesses riches of sensations and a wealth of rapture
that surpass the intensest joys of brilliant day, shedding
behind them a radiance that penetrates the brightest daylight
as sunshine penetrates an electrically lighted hall, – I began
to pay more attention to my dreams and, especially in dreary
joyless days, to look forward to the nights in which I had
unmistakably felt the shining presence of such great treasure.

As to the doctors' opinion regarding the morbidness of
dreams, I refer again to my observations on the Philistinism
prevalent among physicians, and I know from very positive
experience that there are healthy as well as morbid sensations in sleep, precisely as in the day-life. I may speak with
some authority because in my day-life I never experienced
any serious morbid disorder and no doctor could ever cast a
doubt on the excellence of my health. Yet for me a dreamless
night is a bad night, and I call the man who passes his days
in the following of perverted and inharmonious impulses,
in deviations from the good instincts for refreshment and
nourishment, for propagation and accumulation, for peace
and happiness, and his nights in dull unconsciousness and
thoughtlessness, dead as a cork, or at most, a little mad
temporarily from foolish and confused dreams, – such a man
I, with good reason, call sickly and abnormal.

For our highest instinct, that like a stately royal stag,
proudly holding aloft his widely branching antlers, should take
the lead of all the wanton and timid flock of our impulses and
passions uniting and guarding them, is the impulse toward
beauty, toward sublimity, and toward purest blessedness.
Even the mighty passion for knowledge, which impels us so
untiringly to seek for the secret of life, is subordinate to this,
though it is the second in rank – the most beautiful hind of the

flock.

And if in our sleep and dreams we perceive, more distinctly than in the day life, signs of the highest beauty and the purest bliss, – should we not then give them our closest attention?

And this I would now point out to you, dear reader, as the first new idea, strange – till now – to the present world, the first thought-child pulsing with life and future promise, born of the profound union of my experience and contemplation:

The solution of the secret of our lives lies in our dreams.

'Les Rêves'
Marquis d'Hervey de Saint-Denys, 1867

French ethnographer the Marquis d'Hervey de Saint-Denys (1822–1892) shared his personal account of lucid dreaming in the book *Dreams and the Ways to Guide Them*. These illustrations are based on Hervey de Saint-Denys's own sketches, documenting visions experienced just before falling asleep.

Mesmeric Experience
Harriet Martineau, 1845

> English journalist and writer Harriet Martineau (1802–1876)
> became an advocate of Mesmeric therapy, which induces
> trance states, after it aided her recovery from a debilitating
> illness. This excerpt is taken from the first of Martineau's
> published *Letters on Mesmerism*.

Another striking incident occurred in one of the earliest of my
walks. My Mesmerist and I had reached a headland nearly half
a mile from home, and were resting there, when she proposed
to mesmerise me a little – partly to refresh me for our return,
and partly to see whether any effect would be produced in a
new place, and while a fresh breeze was blowing. She merely
laid her hand on my forehead, and, in a minute or two the
usual appearances came, assuming a strange air of novelty
from the scene in which I was. After the blurring of the
outlines, which made all objects more dim than the dull grey
day had already made them, the phosphoric lights appeared,
glorifying every rock and headland, the horizon, and all the
vessels in sight. One of the dirtiest and meanest of the steam
tugs in the port was passing at the time, and it was all dressed
in heavenly radiance – the last object that any imagination
would select as an element of a vision. Then, and often before
and since, did it occur to me that if I had been a pious and very
ignorant Catholic, I could not have escaped the persuasion that
I had seen heavenly visions. Every glorified object before my
open eyes would have been a revelation; and my Mesmerist,
with the white halo round her head, and the illuminated
profile, would have been a saint or an angel.

Sometimes the induced darkening has been so great, that I
have seriously inquired whether the lamp was not out, when a
few movements of the head convinced me that it was burning

as brightly as ever. As the muscular power oozes away under the mesmeric influence, a strange inexplicable feeling ensues of the frame becoming transparent and ductile. My head has often appeared to be drawn out, to change its form, according to the traction of my Mesmerist; and an indescribable and exceedingly agreeable sensation of transparency and lightness, through a part or the whole of the frame, has followed. Then begins the moaning, of which so much has been made, as an indication of pain. I have often moaned, and much oftener have been disposed to do so, when the sensations have been the most tranquil and agreeable. At such times, my Mesmerist has struggled not to disturb me by a laugh, when I have murmured with a serious tone, "Here are my hands, but they have no arms to them:" "O dear! What shall I do? Here is none of me left!" the intellect and moral powers being all the while at their strongest. Between this condition and the mesmeric sleep there is a state, transient and rare, of which I have had experience, but of which I intend to give no account. A somnambule calls it a glimmering of the lights of somnambulism and clairvoyance. To me there appears nothing like glimmering in it. The ideas that I have snatched from it, and now retain, are, of all ideas which ever visited me, the most lucid and impressive. It may be well that they are incommunicable – partly from their nature and relations, and partly from their unfitness for translation into mere words. I will only say that the condition is one of no 'nervous excitement,' as far as experience and outward indications can be taken as a test. Such a state of repose, of calm translucent intellectuality, I had never conceived of; and no reaction followed, no excitement but that which is natural to every one who finds himself in possession of a great new idea.

'Animal Magnetism'
Unknown artist, 1815

In this satirical representation of 'animal magnetism' –
Franz Mesmer's (1734–1815) term for the trance therapy that
later took his name – the patient lies asleep beside a copy of
Ovid's *Metamorphoses*.

Thierischer Magnetismus.

Eine ernste Beschäftigung für tiefe Denker und gläubige Gemüther.

The Clairvoyant or, the Sleepwalker
Gustave Courbet, *c*.1865

The title of French painter Gustave Courbet's (1819–1877) arresting work links sleepwalking with a supernatural ability to see into the future.

Sleep-Waking
John Elliotson, 1835

Three years after publishing these passages in *Human Physiology*, English physician John Elliotson (1791–1868) resigned from his post at University College London, following the outlawing of his Mesmeric practices.

I saw the sleep-waking condition strikingly exhibited lately in a patient of mine in University College Hospital, – a girl, sixteen years of age, destitute of the sense of smell as long as she could remember, subject to pain of her vertex, and, like her sister, epileptic, though very intelligent, very facetious, and of excellent behaviour. After the Baron Dupotet, passing the ends of his fingers up and down before her, had sent her to sleep, on many occasions, for a few minutes at a time, she was observed one day suddenly to talk unconnectedly and move her arms and hands about, though incapable of hearing, seeing, or feeling. She lay in bed or sat, with her eyes open, saying a great number of things, such as she might say when awake, told stories, and with great expression of voice, features, and manner, mimicked the voices and conversation of many fellow-patients accurately, and mimicked the manipulations of Baron Dupotet; yet she saw nobody, could not be roused by hallooing in her ear, and bore the sharpest pinches with indifference. She was cross, expressed displeasure at having before been magnetised, said she would not be made a fool of, complained of different things, shook her head, moving it forwards and frowning, and saying, "You dirty beast." Her hands were very cold in such attacks, and her whole surface pale. She would suddenly come out of this state, stare about like a person waking, rub her eyes, become still, smile, and be completely herself without the least knowledge of what she had been doing, and feel quite ashamed and beg pardon,

MESMERISM | SLEEPWALKING

when informed that she had said we made a fool of her. After some hours, or days, the attack would return. But, before she remained permanently awake, she sometimes fell back repeatedly into the sleep-waking: and nothing could be more striking than to see her eyes suddenly fixed unconsciously, and then all the phenomena of perfect external insensibility and talking begin again in less than a minute: and, in a few minutes, to observe her become suddenly still, look wild or fall fast asleep for an instant, rub her eyes, be sentient of every thing around her, smile, and in short in less than a minute be wide awake, without any knowledge of the state in which she had just been.

An Account of Jane C Rider, The Springfield Somnambulist
L W Belden, 1834

> American physician Lemuel Whittlesey Belden (1801–1839) described somnambulism, or sleepwalking, as "the connecting link between dreaming and insanity". Here, Belden observes the actions of a 17-year-old girl while she sleeps.

Having dressed herself, she went down stairs, and proceeded to make preparations for breakfast. She set the table, arranged the various articles with the utmost precision, went into a dark room and to a closet at the most remote corner, from which she took the coffee cups, placed them on a waiter, turned it sideways to pass through the doors, avoided all intervening obstacles, and deposited the whole safely on the table.

She then went into the pantry, the blinds of which were shut, and the door closed after her. She there skimmed the milk, poured the cream into one cup and the milk into another without spilling a drop. She then cut the bread, placed it regularly on the plate, and divided the slices in the middle. In fine, she went through the whole operation of preparing breakfast with as much precision as she could in open day; and this with her eyes closed, and without any light except that of one lamp which was standing in the breakfast room to enable the family to observe her operations. During the whole time, she seemed to take no notice of those around her, unless they purposely stood in her way, or placed chairs or other obstacles before her, when she avoided them, with an expression of impatience at being thus disturbed.

She finally returned voluntarily to bed, and on finding the table arranged for breakfast when she made her appearance in the morning, inquired why she had been suffered to sleep, while another had performed her duty. None of the transactions of the preceding night had left the slightest impression on her mind – a sense of fatigue the following day being the only evidence furnished by her consciousness in confirmation of the testimony of those who saw her.

After this the paroxysms became more frequent, a week seldom passing without her getting up two or three times. Sometimes she did not leave her room, but was occupied in looking over the contents of her trunk, and arranging the different articles of dress. She occasionally placed things where she could not find them when awake, but some circumstances induced the belief that the knowledge of their situation was restored to her in a subsequent paroxysm. In one instance she disposed of her needlebook where she could not afterwards discover it; but after some time had elapsed, she was found one night in her chamber, sewing a ring on the curtain with a needle which she must have procured from the lost book.

The entire paroxysm was sometimes passed in bed, where she sung, talked, and repeated passages of poetry. Once she imagined herself at Brattleborough, spoke of scenes and persons with which she was acquainted there, and described the characters of certain individuals with great accuracy and shrewdness, and imitated their actions so exactly as to produce a most comical effect. At this time she denied ever having been at Springfield, nor could she be made to recollect a single individual with whom she was acquainted here, except one or two whom she had known in Brattleborough. Even the name of the people with whom she lived seemed unfamiliar and strange to her.

The Somnambulatory Butcher
An Episode
Anonymous, 1821

These verses follow the fate of a man whose legs, "without the sanction of the brain, were fond to wander on the midnight plain".

But he had failings, as I said before,
So, duly as his nose began to snore,
His legs ran with his body to the door;
And forth he used to roam, with sidelong neck,
To – as the Scots folk term it – lift the sneck.
All in his short and woollen cap he strayed,
Silent, though dreaming; cold, but undismay'd.
The moon was shining mid the depth of Heaven,
And from the chill north, fleecy clouds were driven
Athwart its silver aspect, till they grew
Dimmer, and dimmer, in the distant blue;
The trees were rustling loud; nor moon, nor trees,
Nor cloud, could on his dreaming phrenzy seize,
But, walking with closed eyes across the street,
He lifted handsomely his unshod feet,

Till nought, at length, his wandering ankles propt,
And head and heels into the pond he dropt.

Then rose the loud lament; the earth and skies
Rung with his shouts, and echoed with his cries;
The neighbours, in their night-caps, throng'd around,
Call'd forth in marching order at the sound;
They haled young Neckum out, a blankey roll'd
Around his limbs with comfortable fold,
Hurried him home, and told him, cursing deep,
'That if again with cries he broke their sleep,
Him they would change into a wandering ghost,
Draw from the pond, but hang him on a post.'

Oh! Reader, learn this truth most firm and sure,
That vicious practices are hard to cure;
That error girds up with a serpent fold,
Hangs on the youth, but clings about the old. –
Night after Night, if rainy, cold, or fair,
Forth went our hero, just to take the air;
Ladies were terrified, and, fainting, cried,
A ghost in white had wander'd by their side!
The soldier home his quaking path pursued,
With hair on end, gun cock'd, and bayonet screw'd,
And frightful children run to bed in fear,
When mothers said the ghost in white was near!

'Twas a hard case, but Theodore's mother quick
Fell on a scheme to cure him of the trick;
Hard by his bed a washing-tub she placed,
So, when he rose, it washed him to the waist;
And loud he roar'd, – while startled at the sound,

Old women bolted from their beds around –
'Save, save a wandering sinner, or he'd drown'd!!!'

He rose no more, as I'm inform'd, in sleep,
But duly fell'd down cows, and slaughter'd sheep,
Took to himself a wife, a pretty wench,
Sold beef by pounds, and cow-heel on a bench;
In ten years had seven boys, and five fair girls,
With cheeks like roses, and with teeth like pearls;
Lay still in bed like any decent man,
Pursued through life a staid, and honest plan,
And lived beloved, while honours thicken'd o'er
    him,
Justice of Peace, and Custos Rotulorum.

So all my readers from this tale may learn,
The right way from the wrong way to discern;
Never by dreams and nonsense to be led,
Walk when they wake, and slumber when in bed!

'Extraordinary Plea of Somnambulism'
Boston Daily Mail, 1846

American shoe manufacturer Albert J Tirrell (1824–1880)
was acquitted of murdering his mistress after his counsel
presented an "extraordinary plea of somnambulism".
This newspaper report reproduces the defence's opening
argument.

You know, gentlemen, that the mind is susceptible of different
changes – different conditions. There is idiocy – ecstasy –
intoxication – ordinary sleep – madness – monomania – and

somnambulism or *sleep-walking* – or *sleep waking* – [...], talking
in a state of unconscious sleep. With some or all of these
states the court and jury are familiar, and know them to be
common. And, gentlemen, should any of you be unfamiliar
with the state and meaning of spontaneous *somnambulism* –
the defence which the defendant sets up in his behalf – should
you be satisfied that a homicide has been committed, and that
he was the author of the deed – I say, should any of the jury be
unfamiliar with the meaning of *somnambulism* – it will only
be necessary to show that this state is like any other *mental
condition* with which you are familiar. Hence, if we show that
it is like a state of *dreaming* – like a state of *intoxication* – like a
state of *insanity* – yea, more, if we show, as we shall be able to
do, that it is a state of real mental derangement – then the case
is divested of all obscurity, and is at once rendered perfectly
intelligible.

The question of *somnambulism*, as it comes up for examin-
ation here, is in no way connected with what is denominated
mesmeric somnambulism – I speak with all respect for the
professors in that art.

Spontaneous somnambulism, or *sleep walking*, or *sleep-waking*,
as it has been more recently denominated by medical writers,
is a diseased state of the mind resulting from certain *nervous
changes* – which have been known and treated of from the
earliest periods of antiquity to the present time. It is a mental
disease – an unsoundness of mind – and however involved
and difficult in theory, of great familiarity in fact.

What, then is *somnambulism*? It is literally walking in one's
sleep – or as the later writers have termed it, sleep walking;
because men in this state, though asleep, perform all or most
of the functions of men awake.

Without entering critically or profoundly into the philosophy of *sleep*, it may be proper for me to remark, by way of
introduction to what shall follow, that, according to the

received notions of learned and approved authors upon the subject – there are distributed over the surface of the human body innumerable minute and delicate *sensitive* and *initiative fibres, originating* from the brain, and branching out therefrom in all directions, and adapted to each of the senses, by means of which a communication is kept up between the *brain* – the tabernacle of the mind – and the remotest extremities of the body. These fibres coming in contact with external objects, become fatigued, exhausted and torpid, in proportion to the length and violence of their exertion, until, by prolonged action, they become utterly inert and ceaseless, and render to the mind no account of what is going on around us. This general torpitude or inaction of all the external senses is called *sleep*. By the exercise of the *will* or any other strong stimulus, this torpitude may be postponed, and by consent of the *will* it may be accelerated. Sometimes it has been observed, that from a diseased state of the constitution, all the organs of external sense do not yield alike to the general torpor of the frame – and the sense of sight, or hearing, or any other sense, may continue awake, or may be roused or stimulated into action in the midst of the soundest sleep, while all the other senses continue torpid, or are plunged in a deeper sleep. In this state of body, one or more of the intellectual, and one or more of the moral faculties may be and often are in a state of activity; and though in these states we may be able to reason correctly in some respects, yet, the activity of our mind being partial, we are unable to discover the incompatibility of the circumstances we fancy to surround us. The mind is fixed on its own impressions as possessing a real and present existence, and is unable by reason to correct the erroneous conceptions. Persons in this state walk, and perform a variety of actions, without hearing, or seeing, or consciousness of their situation.

3: Language | Memory

Language acquisition | *Memory* |
Power of speech | *Loss of speech*
| Inner voice | *Mental imagery* | Slips
of the tongue | *Aphasia* | Memory loss
| *Recollecting* | Forgetting | *The self* |
Lost memory | *Amnesia* | Forgetfulness
| *Sensory memory* | Mnemonics |
Synaesthesia | False memories
| *Memory construction* | Implanted
memories | *Hypnosis* | Trauma
memories

The Dumb House
John Burnside, 1997

> The narrator of Scottish poet John Burnside's (b. 1955) first
> novel attempts to find the "locus of the soul" by experimen-
> ting on his own children. In this excerpt he recalls his own
> early experience of language and a formative bedtime story.

From the moment I first learned to talk, I felt I was being
tricked out of something. I remember it still – the memory
is clear and indisputable: I am standing in the garden, and
Mother is saying the word *rose* over and over, reciting it like a
magic spell and pointing to the blossoms on the trellis, sugar-
pink and slightly overblown – and I am listening, watching her
lips move, still trying to disconnect the flower from the sound.
I was already too old to be learning to talk – maybe two, or
getting on for three. For a long time, I refused to speak – or so
Mother told me. Though I appeared intelligent in other ways, I
had problems with language. She had even gone to the doctor
about it, but he had told her such things happened, it was
quite normal, I would learn to talk sooner or later, in my own
time, and I would quickly make up the ground I had lost. He
was right. When I did begin speaking, it was a kind of capitu-
lation, as if a tension in my body had broken, and I spoke my
first word that afternoon, the word *rose*, meaning that pink,
fleshy thing that suddenly flared out from the indescribable
continuum of my world, and became an object.

The trick and the beauty of language is that it seems to
order the whole universe, misleading us into believing that
we live in sight of a rational space, a possible harmony. But if
words distance us from the present, so we never quite seize
the reality of things, they make an absolute fiction of the past.
Now, when I look back, I remember a different world: what
must have seemed random and chaotic at the time appears

perfectly logical as I tell it, invested with a clarity that even
suggests a purpose, a meaning to life. I remember the country
around our house as it was before they built the new estates:
a dense, infinite darkness filled with sheltering birds and
holly trees steeped in the Fifties. I remember the old village:
children going from house to house in white sheets, singing
and laughing in the dark, waving to us as our car glided by.
I remember those months of being alone here, after Mother
died. At night, when the land was quiet and still, I would take
off my clothes and go naked from room to room, then out into
the cool moonlight, wandering amongst the flower beds like
an animal, or a changeling from one of Mother's fairy stories.
The garden is walled on all sides; no one could see me, and the
house was so far from the village that I would hear nothing
but the owls in the woods, and the occasional barking of foxes
out on the meadow. Sometimes I wondered if I was real – my
body would be different, clothed in its own sticky-sweet smell,
a smell like sleep, laced with Chanel No.19 from Mother's
dressing table.

   When I was a child, Mother would come into the bedroom
and tell me stories. It was a ritual she performed, without
variation: I had to go up to bed, and she would follow five
minutes later. I would hear the clock strike nine as she climbed
the stairs. Sometimes she brought a book, but quite often she
told me the stories out of her head. Whether she made them
up, or had them by heart, I couldn't say, but she never once
hesitated or filtered. I had the impression, then, that she knew
every story that had ever been told, and all she had to do was
think of one for a moment, and every detail came flooding into
her mind, instantly. It was Mother who told me the story of
Akbar: how he built the Dumb House, not for profit, or even to
prove a point, but from pure curiosity. Nobody knows how long
it stood, or what happened to the children who were locked
inside with their mute attendants. Nobody knows because the

story of the Dumb House was only ever an episode in another, much longer story, an anecdote that had been folded in, told in passing to illustrate the personality of Akbar the Mughal, the dyslexic emperor whose collection of manuscripts was the richest in the known world. Later I realised that most of the details of the story were embellishments that Mother had added herself, to spin out this single episode that I liked so much. In fact, the original story of the Dumb House was simple and fleeting. In that version, the Mughal's counsellors were debating whether a child is born with the innate, God-given ability to speak; they had agreed this gift is equivalent in some way to the soul, the one characteristic that marks out the human from the animal. But Akbar declared that speech is learned, for the very reason that the soul is innate, and the soul does not correspond to any single faculty, whether it be the ability to speak, or to dream, or to reason. Surely, he argued, if speech came from the soul, then there would be only one language, instead of many. But the counsellors disagreed. While it was true that there were many languages, these were simply the corruptions of the original gift, implanted in the soul by God. They knew of incidents in which children had been left in isolation for years, or raised by animals: in such circumstances they had created a language of their own, that nobody else understood, which they could not have learned from others.

Akbar listened. When the counsellors had finished speaking, he told them he would test their hypothesis. He had his craftsmen build a mansion, far from the city: a large, well-appointed house, with its own gardens and fountains. Here Akbar established a court of the mute, into which he introduced a number of new-born babies, gathered from the length and breadth of the Empire. The children were well cared for, and were provided with everything they could possibly need, but because their attendants were dumb, they never heard human speech, and they grew up unable to talk, as Akbar had predicted. People would travel from all over the kingdom to visit the house. They would stand for hours outside its walled gardens, listening to the silence, and for years to come the mansion was known as the Gang Mahal, or Dumb House.

Mother would come to the bedroom and tell me this story in the evenings. Naturally, her version was different; she barely touched upon the controversy over the innateness of language, or the nature of the soul. Instead she described the Gang Mahal in sumptuous detail: the orange trees in terracotta pots, the jewelled walls, the unearthly silence. I lay in bed listening, watching her lips move, intoxicated by her perfume. I used to wonder what had happened when those children grew up; how they thought, if thought was possible, if they ever remembered anything from one moment to the next. There are people who say speech is magical; for them, words have the power to create and destroy. Listening to Mother's stories, I became enmeshed in a view of the world: an expectation, a secret fear. Even now, nothing seems more beautiful to me than language when it creates the impression of order; the naming of things after their true nature; the act of classification; the creation of kingdoms and genera, species and sub-species; the designation of animal, vegetable or mineral, of monocotyledonous plants, freshwater fishes, birds of prey, the periodic table. This is why the past seems perfect, a time of proportion and order, because it is immersed in speech. For animals, memory might reside as a sensation, a resonance in the nerves, or in the meat of the spine. But for humans, the past cannot be described except in words. It is nowhere else. What disturbs me now is the possibility that language might fail: after the experiment ended so inconclusively, I cannot help imagining that the order which seems inherent in things is only a construct, that everything might fall into chaos, somewhere in the long white reaches of forgetting.

'The Gang Mahal'
Abu'l-Fazl, 1590s

> The Gang Mahal experiment appears in the official history
> of the Mughal emperor Akbar (1542–1605). Akbar believed
> that the children raised in the 'dumb-house' communicated
> "with a tongueless tongue".

In the 24th Divine year [His Majesty] said that speech came
to every tribe from hearing, and that each remembered from
another from the beginning of existence. If they arranged that
human speech did not reach them, they certainly would not
have the power of speech. If the fountain of speech bubbled
over in one of them, he would regard this as Divine speech,
and accept it as such. As some who heard this appeared to
deny it, he, in order to convince them, had a *serai* [palace] built
in a place which civilised sounds did not reach. The newly born
were put into that place of experience, and honest and active
guards were put over them. For a time tongue-tied (*zabān
basta*) wetnurses were admitted there. As they had closed
the door of speech, the place was commonly called the Gang
Mahal (the dumb-house). On the 29th (Amardād – 9th August
1582) he went out to hunt. That night he stayed in Faiẓābād,
and next day he went with a few special attendants to the house
of experiment. No cry came from that house of silence, nor
was any speech heard there. In spite of their four years they
had no part of the talisman of speech, and nothing came out
except the noise of the dumb.

SPEECH ACQUISITION

A Report to an Academy
Franz Kafka, 1917

> In this fictional presentation by Franz Kafka (1883–1924)
> the speaker recounts his "previous life as an ape". Despite
> successfully mimicking the behaviour of men, the ape views
> speech as the true measure of being human.

It was so easy to imitate these people. I could already spit on the first day. Then we used to spit in each other's faces. The only difference was that I licked my face clean afterwards. They did not. Soon I was smoking a pipe, like an old man, and if I then pressed my thumb down into the bowl of the pipe, the entire area between decks cheered. Still, for a long time I did not understand the difference between an empty and a full pipe.

I had the greatest difficulty with the bottle of alcohol. The smell was torture to me. I forced myself with all my power, but weeks went by before I could overcome my reaction. Curiously enough, the people took this inner struggle more seriously than anything else about me. In my memories I don't distinguish the people, but there was one who always came back, alone or with comrades, day and night, at all hours. He'd stand with the bottle in front of me and give me instructions. He did not understand me. He wanted to solve the riddle of my being. He used to uncork the bottle slowly and then look at me, in order to test if I had understood. I confess that I always looked at him with wildly over-eager attentiveness. No human teacher has ever found in the entire earthly globe such a student of human beings. After he'd uncorked the bottle, he'd raise it to his mouth. I'd gaze at him, right into his throat. He would nod, pleased with me, and set the bottle to his lips. Delighted with my gradual understanding, I'd squeal and scratch myself all over, wherever it was convenient. He was happy. He'd set

the bottle to his mouth and take a swallow. Impatient and
desperate to emulate him, I would defecate over myself in
my cage – and that again gave him great satisfaction. Then,
holding the bottle at arm's length and bringing it up once more
with a swing, he'd drink it down with one gulp, exaggerating
his backward bending as a way of instructing me. Exhausted
with so much great effort, I could no longer follow and would
hang weakly onto the bars, while he ended the theoretical
lesson by rubbing his belly and grinning.

Now the practical exercises first began. Was I not already
too tired out by the theoretical part? Yes, indeed, far too weary.
That's part of my fate. Nonetheless, I'd grab the proffered
bottle as well as I could and uncork it trembling. Once I'd
managed to do that, a new energy would gradually take over. I
lifted the bottle – with hardly any difference between me and
the original – put it to my lips – and throw it away in disgust,
in disgust, although it was empty and filled only with the
smell, throw it with disgust onto the floor. To the sorrow of my
teacher, to my own greater sorrow. And I still did not console
him or myself when, after throwing away the bottle, I did not
forget to give my belly a splendid rub and to grin as I do so.

All too often, the lesson went that way. And to my teacher's
credit, he was not angry with me. Well, sometimes he held his
burning pipe against my fur in some place or other which I
could reach only with difficulty, until it began to burn. But
then he would put it out himself with his huge good hand.
He wasn't angry with me. He realised that we were fighting
on the same side against ape nature and that I had the more
difficult part.

It was certainly a victory for him when one evening in front
of a large circle of onlookers – perhaps it was a celebration, a
gramophone was playing, an officer was wandering around
among the people – when on this evening, at a moment when
no one was watching, I grabbed a bottle of alcohol which had

been inadvertently left standing in front of my cage, uncorked it just as I had been taught, amid the rising attention of the group, set it against my mouth and, without hesitating, with my mouth making no grimace, like an expert drinker, with my eyes rolling around, splashing the liquid in my throat, I really and truly drank the bottle empty, and then threw it away, no longer in despair, but like an artist. Well, I did forget to scratch my belly. But instead of that, because I couldn't do anything else, because I had to, because my senses were roaring, I cried out a short and good "Hello!" breaking out into human sounds. And with this cry I sprang into the community of human beings, and I felt its echo – "Just listen. He's talking!" – like a kiss on my entire sweat-soaked body.

The Mark of the Beast
Rudyard Kipling, 1890

> Rudyard Kipling's (1865–1936) horror story tells the tale of
> three friends in India. This incident occurs the morning after
> Fleete has been manhandled by "a silver leper". Fleete's
> loss of speech is the final stage in a transformation beyond
> the human.

Strickland sat with me in the stables and asked if I had noticed anything peculiar in Fleete's manner. I said that he ate his food like a beast; but that this might have been the result of living alone in the hills out of the reach of society as refined and elevating as ours for instance. Strickland was not amused. I do not think that he listened to me, for his next sentence referred to the mark on Fleete's breast, and I said that it might have been caused by blister-flies, or that it was possibly a birth-mark newly born and now visible for the first time. We both agreed that it was unpleasant to look at, and Strickland found occasion to say that I was a fool.

"I can't tell you what I think now," said he, "because you would call me a madman; but you must stay with me for the next few days, if you can. I want you to watch Fleete, but don't tell me what you think till I have made up my mind."

"But I am dining out to-night," I said.

"So am I," said Strickland, "and so is Fleete. At least if he doesn't change his mind."

We walked about the garden smoking, but saying nothing – because we were friends, and talking spoils good tobacco – till our pipes were out. Then we went to wake up Fleete. He was wide awake and fidgeting about his room.

"I say, I want some more chops," he said. "Can I get them?"

We laughed and said, "Go and change. The ponies will be round in a minute."

"All right," said Fleete. "I'll go when I get the chops – underdone ones, mind."

He seemed to be quite in earnest. It was four o'clock, and we had had breakfast at one; still, for a long time, he demanded those underdone chops. Then he changed into riding clothes and went out into the verandah. His pony – the mare had not been caught – would not let him come near. All three horses were unmanageable – mad with fear – and finally Fleete said that he would stay at home and get something to eat. Strickland and I rode out wondering. As we passed the temple of Hanuman, the Silver Man came out and mewed at us.

"He is not one of the regular priests of the temple," said Strickland. "I think I should peculiarly like to lay my hands on him."

There was no spring in our gallop on the racecourse that evening. The horses were stale, and moved as though they had been ridden out.

"The fright after breakfast has been too much for them,"

said Strickland.

That was the only remark he made through the remainder of the ride. Once or twice I think he swore to himself; but that did not count.

We came back in the dark at seven o'clock, and saw that there were no lights in the bungalow. "Careless ruffians my servants are!" said Strickland.

My horse reared at something on the carriage drive, and Fleete stood up under its nose.

"What are you doing, grovelling about the garden?" said Strickland.

But both horses bolted and nearly threw us. We dismounted by the stables and returned to Fleete, who was on his hands and knees under the orange-bushes.

"What the devil's wrong with you?" said Strickland.

"Nothing, nothing in the world," said Fleete, speaking very quickly and thickly. "I've been gardening – botanising you know. The smell of the earth is delightful. I think I'm going for a walk – a long walk – all night."

Then I saw that there was something excessively out of order somewhere, and I said to Strickland, "I am not dining out."

"Bless you!" said Strickland. "Here, Fleete, get up. You'll catch fever there. Come in to dinner and let's have the lamps lit. We'll all dine at home."

Fleete stood up unwillingly, and said, "No lamps – no lamps. It's much nicer here. Let's dine outside and have some more chops – lots of 'em and underdone – bloody ones with gristle."

Now a December evening in Northern India is bitterly cold, and Fleete's suggestion was that of a maniac.

"Come in," said Strickland sternly. "Come in at once."

Fleete came, and when the lamps were brought, we saw that he was literally plastered with dirt from head to foot.

He must have been rolling in the garden. He shrank from the light and went to his room. His eyes were horrible to look at. There was a green light behind them, not in them, if you understand, and the man's lower lip hung down.

Strickland said, "There is going to be trouble – big trouble – tonight. Don't you change your riding-things."

We waited and waited for Fleete's reappearance, and ordered dinner in the meantime. We could hear him moving about his own room, but there was no light there. Presently from the room came the long-drawn howl of a wolf.

People write and talk lightly of blood running cold and hair standing up and things of that kind. Both sensations are too horrible to be trifled with. My heart stopped as though a knife had been driven through it, and Strickland turned as white as the tablecloth.

The howl was repeated, and was answered by another howl far across the fields.

That set the gilded roof on the horror. Strickland dashed into Fleete's room. I followed, and we saw Fleete getting out of the window. He made beast-noises in the back of his throat. He could not answer us when we shouted at him. He spat.

I don't quite remember what followed, but I think that Strickland must have stunned him with the long boot-jack or else I should never have been able to sit on his chest. Fleete could not speak, he could only snarl, and his snarls were those of a wolf, not of a man. The human spirit must have been giving way all day and have died out with the twilight. We were dealing with a beast that had once been Fleete.

What Does Your Inner Voice Sound Like?
Jennifer Hodgson, 2015

> The Writers' Inner Voices project attempts to understand
> writers' and storytellers' inner speech and the role the inner
> voice, or voices, play in the process of literary creation. This
> blog post explores how the inner, or thought, voice links
> with mental imagery.

Try it for yourself: stop what you're doing and try to listen in
to the mind's ear. What can you hear? Indeed, are you hearing
at all? Can you say, definitively, that your inner voice *sounds* in
the sense that we usually understand it? If not, how are you
perceiving what it is that you're experiencing? Now try to
describe this inner voice. Are you able to put into words what
it feels like to 'tune in' to the voice you hear in your head – if,
indeed, you are *hearing* it at all?

The inner voice is a very common aspect of most of our
lives. Although a small minority of people claim never to
experience it, the vast majority of us are very familiar with
the clamour of voices that make up the mind's chatter. At any
one time, that voice may be distinctly your own: rehearsing a
dreaded talk with your boss, or chastising yourself for forgetting an important appointment. But you might just as easily
recognise it as the voice of a parent, a celebrity, an old friend
or a much-loved schoolteacher. Such self-talk is an example of
what philosophers and psychologists call 'mental imagery', an
experience which resembles a perceptual experience but lacks
any source of sensory input. As [Denise] Riley comments[1]...
despite our familiarity with what we might call 'hearing in the
head', there are far more ways of talking about *visual* experiences of this kind than there are *auditory* ones – hence why
we use the term 'imagery' to denote the broad gamut of
'quasi-sensory' experiences that occur in our minds.

We talk of 'picturing in our mind's eye' for example, or of 'visualising', or of 'having an image in our head'. But beyond the auditory experiences with which we are specifically concerned here, it is very likely that similar experiences in other sensory modes (or, indeed, combinations thereof) are just as common: motor imagery, haptic imagery and olfactory imagery, for example.

Pinning down precisely the nature and function of auditory mental imagery has long been the subject of debates amongst philosophers, psychologists and cognitive neuroscientists. And this challenge of knowing what we mean when we talk about our inner voices also arose during our interviews with writers at the 2014 Edinburgh International Book Festival. We asked them the same questions we posed to you at the top of this blog post. And it seems that describing exactly what their inner voices sounded like (if indeed they sounded at all) and how it felt to experience them taxed even veteran writers' well-honed powers of description. Here's a sample of their responses:

This writer doubts whether the 'thought voice' is verbal at all. Perhaps, they ponder, the content of the mind only becomes encased in words when we attend to it:

I think it's just a thought voice. A voice of thought; it's not a voice of words. I suppose, when you pay attention to it, I suppose it's a bit like meditation in a way, you focus on something. You focus and then the words come. So it's almost like the old days when you used to develop photographs in a dark room and the image would emerge, it's like that.

This one insists that in general they don't have an inner voice, but then modifies their first comment to explain that their inner voice is not a discordant one. They also describe 'hearing' the voices of their loved ones:

I don't have an inner voice. My inner voice is not at all different from my outer voice. I don't spend a lot of time thinking x and saying y. I will occasionally hear the voice of one of my late parents, or a teacher I was very close to.

For this writer, the inner voice 'doesn't sound like anything'. Its quality seems to lie somewhere between 'hearing' and 'seeing':

This is very odd; in a weird kind of way it doesn't sound at all... I'm saying I'm hearing a voice but I can't actually tell you what it sounds like. And if you pushed me on that I'd probably say it doesn't sound like anything, it doesn't actually sound like I'm hearing but I am hearing it. It's like it's a silent voice, but it's not like I'm seeing text, so there's something going on. But it's not, I'm hearing it rather than seeing it, but I'm not actually hearing a definite loud voice. That's about the only way I can describe it...

This writer invokes the observer effect to describe why the inner voice is so elusive:

Does it speak in complete sentences? I have no idea... I never even think about it. And even now I couldn't tell you, even though I've been asked the question because I think thinking about it changes it. So, I can't say.

And finally, this writer describes the kind of inner voice that is probably familiar to many of us:

I don't know... It is a really hard question to answer. I mean I have a really rich inner life all the time... I think the days that I just don't ever talk to myself are kind of wasted days...
I am talking to myself all the time, and sometimes all that mundane stuff, just I have to check my email or I wonder are the kids up, or what time does Tesco close, you know.

1 In Riley D. 'A voice without a mouth': inner speech. Qui Parle 2004;14(2):57–104.

Examples of Mistakes in Speech
Sigmund Freud, 1901

In the fifth chapter of his book *Psychopathology of Everyday Life* Austrian psychoanalyst Sigmund Freud (1856–1939) shared numerous examples of mistakes in speech, or slips of the tongue. The publication is thought to be the inspiration for the term 'Freudian slip'.

(a) Seeing my daughter make an unpleasant face while biting into an apple, I wished to quote the following couplet: –

'The ape he is a funny sight,

When in the apple he takes a bite.'

But I began: "The apel..." This seems to be a contamination of 'ape' and 'apple' (compromise formation), or it may be also conceived as an anticipation of the prepared 'apple.' The true state of affairs, however, was this: I began the quotation once before, and made no mistake the first time. I made the mistake only during the repetition, which was necessary because my daughter, having been distracted from another side, did not listen to me. This repetition with the added impatience to disburden myself of the sentence I must include in the motivation of the speech-blunder, which represented itself as a function of condensation.

(b) My daughter said, "I wrote to Mrs Schresinger." The woman's name was Schlesinger. This speech-blunder may depend on the tendency to facilitate articulation. I must state, however, that this mistake was made by my daughter a few moments after I had said *apel* instead of *ape*. Mistakes in speech are in a great measure contagious; a similar peculiarity was noticed by Meringer and Mayer in the forgetting of names. I know of no reason for this psychic contagiousness.

(c) "I *sut* up like a pocket-knife," said a patient in the beginning of treatment, instead of "I *shut* up." This suggests
a difficulty of articulation which may serve as an excuse
for the interchanging of sounds. When her attention
was called to the speech-blunder, she promptly replied,
"Yes, that happened because you said *'earnesht'* instead
of *'earnest.'*" As a matter of fact I received her with the
remark, "To-day we shall be in earnest" (because it was
the last hour before her discharge from treatment), and I
jokingly changed the word into *earnesht*. In the course of
the hour she repeatedly made mistakes in speech, and I
finally observed that it was not only because she imitated
me but because she had a special reason in her unconscious to linger at the word earnest (Ernst) as a name[1].

(d) A woman, speaking about a game invented by her children
and called by them "the man in the box," said "the manx
in the boc." I could readily understand her mistake. It
was while analysing her dream, in which her husband
is depicted as very generous in money matters – just the
reverse of reality – that she made this speech-blunder. The
day before she had asked for a new set of furs, which her
husband denied her, claiming that he could not afford to
spend so much money. She upbraided him for his stinginess, "for putting away so much into the strong-box," and
mentioned a friend whose husband has not nearly his
income, and yet he presented his wife with a *mink* coat for
her birthday. The mistake is now comprehensible. The
word *manx* (*manks*) reduces itself to the 'minks' which she
longs for, and the box refers to her husband's stinginess.

(e) A similar mechanism is shown in the mistake of another
patient whose memory deserted her in the midst of a
long-forgotten childish reminiscence. Her memory failed

to inform her on what part of the body the prying and lustful hand of another had touched her. Soon thereafter she visited one of her friends, with whom she discussed summer homes. Asked where her cottage in M. was located, she answered, "Near the *mountain loin*" instead of "*mountain lane.*"

(*f*) Another patient, whom I asked at the end of her visit how her uncle was, answered: "I don't know, I only see him now *in flagranti.*"

The following day she said, "I am really ashamed of myself for having given you yesterday such a stupid answer. Naturally you must have thought me a very uneducated person who always mistakes the meaning of foreign words. I wished to say *en passant.*" We did not know at the time where she got the incorrectly used foreign words, but during the same session she reproduced a reminiscence as a continuation of the theme from the previous day, in which being caught *in flagranti* played the principal part. The mistake of the previous day had therefore anticipated the recollection, which at that time had not yet become conscious.

(*g*) In discussing her summer plans, a patient said, "I shall remain most of the summer in *Elberlon.*" She noted her mistake, and asked me to analyse it. The associations to *Elberlon* elicited: seashore on the Jersey coast – summer resort – vacation travelling. This recalled travelling in Europe with her cousin, a topic which we had discussed the day before during the analysis of a dream. The dream dealt with her dislike for this cousin, and she admitted that it was mainly due to the fact that the latter was the favourite of the man whom they met together while travelling abroad. During the dream analysis she could not recall the name of the city in which they met this man, and I did not make any effort at the time to bring it to her consciousness, as we were engrossed in a totally different problem. When asked to focus her attention again on Elberlon and reproduce her associations, she said, "It brings to mind *Elberlawn – lawn – field –* and *Elberfield.*" *Elberfeld* was the lost name of the city in Germany. Here the mistake served to bring to consciousness in a concealed manner a memory which was connected with a painful feeling.

1 It turned out that she was under the influence of unconscious thoughts concerning pregnancy and prevention of conception. With the words "shut up like a pocket knife," which she uttered consciously as a complaint, she meant to describe the position of the child in the womb. The word "earnest" in my remark recalled to her the name (S. Ernst) of the well-known Vienna business firm in Karthner Strasse, which used to advertise the sale of articles for the prevention of conception.

Speech Amnesia
Johann A P Gesner, 1770

German physician Johann Gesner (1738–1801) summarised the "uncommon" case of Mr 'KD' a year after the 73-year-old first exhibited a speech impairment. Gesner published this report under the title 'Sprachamnesie', or 'Speech amnesia'.

The words which Herr KD pronounces are for the most part meaningless sounds. However, their total number is not very great, in that a meaningless word is often repeated successively and only occasionally replaced by others which are equally incomprehensible. These sounds sometimes disappear completely and one does not hear them any more; instead, new coinages appear which last a longer or shorter time. For example, the sound 'began', without fixed meaning, which occurred constantly at the beginning of the illness is no longer

APHASIA

uttered a half-year later. Instead, one hears a newly created word, 'Zettejuset' or 'Zettennoset', countless times during the course of a day. Numerals, such as 40, 50, 60, 70, 80, 90, which he uses to serve him in the course of speech, are also to be added to this category.

Doubtlessly these sounds are not always associated with the same ideas for him. They express, or at least are intended to express, all those ideas which he wishes to communicate with others. Their total number is scarcely 100. Thus his currently favourite word 'Zettejuset' can mean more than 1000 things. It is also used by him indiscriminately and mixed up with other words in such a manner that his speech is incomprehensible.

At the same time there also occur occasional meaningful words which for the most part concern only familiar things and are not always within the power of the speaker. Examples are such expressions as 'obedient servant', 'most humble servant', 'good morning', 'I do not wish to', and several other similar expressions which had always characteristically been used by this man of choleric temperament, as well as swear words such as, 'Oh God; Oh God' and 'Damn Foolishness', whereby he indicates his futile efforts.

For the most part he uses these words in their proper meaning. However, I have also observed that if I drink to his health and he wants to thank me, the word, 'Adieu', is brought forth instead of the usual formula. He is likely to say 'Good evening' in the morning and 'Good morning' in the evening involuntarily. Thus in a quite special sense he seems to have lost complete control of his tongue.

Writing and speaking are equally defective. He cannot write his full name even once. When he tries to write something else (which he seldom does because he is aware of his incapacity) he produces words on paper which are as incomprehensible as those he utters.

Nor can he read. These signs of ideas make no impression

on him although other more concrete objects arouse the appropriate concepts in him. It is just this circumstance about which the patient, who always found great pleasure in reading, often complains.

Objects, when they are of an external sensory nature, certainly arouse the correspondingly correct ideas in him. The patient recognises everyone whom he knew before, asks about the circumstances of people with whom he has associated, makes observations about them in accordance with their status, age, sex, etc., and, as has always been characteristic of him, praises, finds fault, or laughs at them (and with justification).

I cannot actually maintain that I have personally observed a loss of certain concepts in him unless such a loss may be inferred from the fact that he does not like to have excerpts from books presenting general spiritual or moral truths read to him. Nor does he pay any attention to them, which seems to show that many abstract concepts may have been lost and can be aroused only with difficulty, if at all, by the external signs which we call words. Otherwise he understands the speech of those around him completely and often to their admiration, unless it is presented in too diffuse a manner or, as mentioned above, concerns abstract matters. Moreover, he can also make his own ideas recognised through external signs and demonstrations to such a degree that, if one guesses the meaning of the signs, they represent quite correct and coherent ideas.

The patient is also aware that he speaks unintelligently and, when he repeats some of these words, has often laughed and joked about it.

Now after a year his condition is essentially as has been described. However, it can be said that, physically and mentally, he has improved rather than got worse. His mental powers have also become stronger, his ideas being more orderly and more definite. A few comprehensible words have also appeared. In brief, after one has observed and spoken with the patient at some length, nothing seems to be wrong with him except his speech. I do not know that I can better make his condition more intelligible and understandable except by saying that if a person who is not acquainted with the German language and who did not know that the patient was sick should observe him and hear him talk, he would take him for a healthy, ordinary man who is speaking an unfamiliar language.

'Syntactical Aphasia'
Henry Head, 1926

> Private Frank Edward S was admitted to the London Hospital with a gunshot wound to the head in 1915. Neurologist Henry Head (1861–1940) employed a range of tests to assess the impact of the soldier's brain injury.

His speech was a perfect example of jargon due to disturbance of rhythm and defective syntax. He did not use wrong words and, if the subject under discussion was known, it was not difficult to gather the meaning of what he said. He tried to 'rush' his phrases and it was difficult to hear the prepositions, conjunctions or articles; these parts of speech were frequently omitted. The same errors marred his attempts to repeat what was said to him or to read aloud; even when reading to himself, he became confused by internal jargon and lost the significance of all but the simplest phrases. His power of naming was preserved, although his nomenclature was sometimes unusual; he could also state the time correctly. On the whole he understood what was said to him, unless he was compelled to repeat it to himself. Simple oral commands were well executed, but he hesitated and made several errors

over more complex tests. His spontaneous writing was poor
and he had little power of reproducing in written words the
contents of a paragraph he had apparently read with understanding. He wrote equally badly to dictation, but could copy
perfectly. In the earlier stages, before the full development of
the fits, he experienced little or no difficulty in counting and
solved simple problems in arithmetic. He could name coins,
knew their relative value and made no mistakes in the use of
money. He evidently appreciated the full meaning of pictures,
but found extreme difficulty in describing them in spoken or
written words. He drew a spirit lamp both from the model and
from memory, but failed to represent an elephant correctly.
Orientation was unaffected and he drew a perfect ground-plan
of a familiar room.

...

Games: He played a perfect game of dominoes and was excellent at bowls.

'Impotence of Memory after Paralysis'
Robert J Graves, 1851

> Irish physician Robert Graves (1796–1853) observed an
> intriguing communication aid compiled by a patient who
> struggled to remember certain parts of speech.

A farmer in the county of Wicklow, in comfortable circumstances, when fifty years of age, had a paralytic fit, in the year
1839; since that time he has never recovered the use of the
affected side, and still labours under a painful degree of hesita-
tion of speech. He is, however, able to walk about, take a great
deal of active exercise, and superintend the business of his
farm. His memory seems to be tolerably good for all parts of
speech except noun-substantives and proper names; the latter

he cannot at all retain; and this defect is accompanied by the following singular peculiarity: that he perfectly recollects the initial letter of every substantive or proper name for which he has occasion in conversation, though he could not recall to his memory the word itself. Experience, therefore, has taught him the utility of having written in manuscript a list of the things he is in the habit of calling for or speaking about, including the proper names of his children, servants, and acquaintances: all these he has arranged alphabetically in a little pocket dictionary, which he uses as follows: if he wishes to ask any thing about a cow, before he commences the sentence he turns to the letter C, and looks out for the word 'cow,' and keeps his finger and eye fixed on the word until he has finished the sentence. He can pronounce the word 'cow' in its proper place, so long as he has his eye fixed upon the written letters; but the moment he shuts the book it passes out of his memory, and cannot be recalled, although he recollects its initial, and can refer to it again when necessary. In the same way when he comes to Dublin, and wishes to consult me (for my name is among the indispensable proper names in his dictionary), he comes with his dictionary open to the hall-door, and asks to see Dr Graves; but, if by accident he has forgotten his dictionary, as happened on one occasion, he is totally unable to tell the servant what or whom he wants. He cannot recollect his own name unless he looks out for it, nor the name of any person of his acquaintance; but he is never for a moment at a loss for the initial which is to guide him in his search for the word he seeks.

His is a remarkably exaggerated degree of the common defect of memory, observed in the diseases of old age, and in which the names of persons and things are frequently forgotten, although their initials are recollected. It is strange that substantives and proper names, words which are the first acquired by the memory in childhood, are sooner forgotten than verbs, adjectives and other parts of speech, which are a much later acquisition.

'Something More Speakingly Incomprehensible'
Jane Austen, 1814

> Memory and memories are persistent themes in English
> novelist Jane Austen's (1775–1817) *Mansfield Park*. Here, the
> main character reflects on the wonderful faculty of memory.

"This is pretty – very pretty," said Fanny, looking around her as
they were thus sitting together one day: "every time I come into
this shrubbery I am more struck with its growth and beauty.
Three years ago, this was nothing but a rough hedgerow along
the upper side of the field, never thought of as anything, or
capable of becoming anything; and now it is converted into a
walk, and it would be difficult to say whether most valuable as
a convenience or an ornament; and perhaps, in another three
years, we may be forgetting – almost forgetting what it was
before. How wonderful, how very wonderful the operations
of time, and the changes of the human mind!" And following
the latter train of thought, she soon afterwards added: "If any
one faculty of our nature may be called more wonderful than
the rest, I do think it is memory. There seems something *more*
speakingly incomprehensible in the powers, the failures, the
inequalities of memory, than in any other of our intelligences.
The memory is sometimes so retentive, so serviceable, so
obedient – at others, so bewildered and so weak – and at others
again, so tyrannic, so beyond controul! – We are, to be sure,
a miracle every way – but our powers of recollecting and of
forgetting do seem peculiarly past finding out."

Miss Crawford, untouched and inattentive, had nothing
to say...

'Remorse Is Memory Awake'
Emily Dickinson, 1863

American poet Emily Dickinson (1830 –1886) personified memory in these verses on remorse, a feeling that requires a division between the later and former self.

Remorse is memory awake,
Her companies astir, –
A presence of departed acts
At window and at door.

Its past set down before the soul,
And lighted with a match,
Perusal to facilitate
Of its condensed despatch.

Remorse is cureless, – the disease
Not even God can heal;
For 'tis His institution, –
The complement of hell.

'The Thief'
Wilkie Collins, 1868

> Amnesia is a common theme in English writer Wilkie
> Collins's (1824–1889) work. This extract from *The
> Moonstone*, commonly viewed as the first English detective
> novel, follows Franklin Blake as he searches for the secret
> hiding place of the lost jewel at the centre of the book's plot.

On our way to the Shivering Sand, I applied to Betteredge to
revive my memory of events (as affecting Rosanna Spearman)
at the period of Sergeant Cuff's inquiry. With my old friend's
help, I soon had the succession of circumstances clearly
registered in my mind. Rosanna's journey to Frizinghall,
when the whole household believed her to be ill in her own
room – Rosanna's mysterious employment of the night-time,
with her door locked, and her candle burning till the morning
– Rosanna's suspicious purchase of the japanned tin case,
and the two dog's chains from Mrs Yolland – the Sergeant's
positive conviction that Rosanna had hidden something at the
Shivering Sand, and the Sergeant's absolute ignorance as to
what that something might be – all these strange results of
the abortive inquiry into the loss of the Moonstone, were
clearly present to me again, when we reached the quicksand,
and walked out together on the low ledge of rocks called the
South Spit.

With Betteredge's help, I soon stood in the right position
to see the Beacon and the Coast-guard flagstaff in a line
together. Following the memorandum as our guide, we next
laid my stick in the necessary direction, as neatly as we could,
on the uneven surface of the rocks. And then we looked at our
watches once more.

It wanted nearly twenty minutes yet of the turn of the
tide. I suggested waiting through this interval on the beach,

instead of on the wet and slippery surface of the rocks. Having reached the dry sand, I prepared to sit down; and, greatly to my surprise, Betteredge prepared to leave me.

"What are you going away for?" I asked.

"Look at the letter again, sir, and you will see."

A glance at the letter reminded me that I was charged, when I made my discovery, to make it alone.

"It's hard enough for me to leave you, at such a time as this," said Betteredge. "But she died a dreadful death, poor soul – and I feel a kind of call on me, Mr Franklin, to humour that fancy of hers. Besides," he added, confidentially, "there's nothing in the letter against your letting out the secret afterwards. I'll hang about in the fir plantation, and wait till you pick me up. Don't be longer than you can help, sir. The detective-fever isn't an easy disease to deal with, under *these* circumstances."

With that parting caution, he left me.

The interval of expectation, short as it was when reckoned by the measure of time, assumed formidable proportions when reckoned by the measure of suspense. This was one of the occasions on which the invaluable habit of smoking becomes especially precious and consolatory. I lit a cigar, and sat down on the slope of the beach.

The sunlight poured its unclouded beauty on every object that I could see. The exquisite freshness of the air made the mere act of living and breathing a luxury. Even the lonely little bay welcomed the morning with a show of cheerfulness; and the bared wet surface of the quicksand itself, glittering with a golden brightness, hid the horror of its false brown face under a passing smile. It was the finest day I had seen since my return to England.

The turn of the tide came, before my cigar was finished. I saw the preliminary heaving of the Sand, and then the awful shiver that crept over its surface – as if some spirit of terror

lived and moved and shuddered in the fathomless deeps
beneath. I threw away my cigar, and went back again to
the rocks.

My directions in the memorandum instructed me to feel
along the line traced by the stick, beginning with the end
which was nearest to the beacon.

I advanced, in this manner, more than half way along
the stick, without encountering anything but the edges of
the rocks. An inch or two further on, however, my patience
was rewarded. In a narrow little fissure, just within reach of
my forefinger, I felt the chain. Attempting, next, to follow
it, by touch, in the direction of the quicksand, I found my
progress stopped by a thick growth of seaweed – which had
fastened itself into the fissure, no doubt, in the time that
had elapsed since Rosanna Spearman had chosen her
hiding-place.

It was equally impossible to pull up the seaweed, or to force
my hand through it. After marking the spot indicated by the
end of the stick which was placed nearest to the quicksand,
I determined to pursue the search for the chain on a plan of
my own. My idea was to 'sound' immediately under the rocks,
on the chance of recovering the lost trace of the chain at the
point at which it entered the sand. I took up the stick, and knelt
down on the brink of the South Spit.

In this position, my face was within a few feet of the
surface of the quicksand. The sight of it so near me, still
disturbed at intervals by its hideous shivering fit, shook my
nerves for the moment. A horrible fancy that the dead woman
might appear on the scene of her suicide, to assist my search
– an unutterable dread of seeing her rise through the heaving
surface of the sand, and point to the place – forced itself into
my mind, and turned me cold in the warm sunlight. I own I
closed my eyes at the moment when the point of the stick first
entered the quicksand.

The instant afterwards, before the stick could have been submerged more than a few inches, I was free from the hold of my own superstitious terror, and was throbbing with excitement from head to foot. Sounding blindfold, at my first attempt – at that first attempt I had sounded right! The stick struck the chain.

Taking a firm hold of the roots of the seaweed with my left hand, I laid myself down over the brink, and felt with my right hand under the overhanging edges of the rock. My right hand found the chain.

I drew it up without the slightest difficulty. And there was the japanned tin case fastened to the end of it.

The action of the water had so rusted the chain, that it was impossible for me to unfasten it from the hasp which attached it to the case. Putting the case between my knees and exerting my utmost strength, I contrived to draw off the cover. Some white substance filled the whole interior when I looked in. I put in my hand, and found it to be linen.

In drawing out the linen, I also drew out a letter crumpled up with it. After looking at the direction, and discovering that it bore my name, I put the letter in my pocket, and completely removed the linen. It came out in a thick roll, moulded, of course, to the shape of the case in which it had been so long confined, and perfectly preserved from any injury by the sea.

I carried the linen to the dry sand of the beach, and there unrolled and smoothed it out. There was no mistaking it as an article of dress. It was a nightgown.

The uppermost side, when I spread it out, presented to view innumerable folds and creases, and nothing more. I tried the undermost side, next – and instantly discovered the smear of the paint from the door of Rachel's boudoir!

My eyes remained riveted on the stain, and my mind took me back at a leap from present to past. The very words of Sergeant Cuff recurred to me, as if the man himself was at my side again, pointing to the unanswerable inference which he drew from the smear on the door.

"Find out whether there is any article of dress in this house with the stain of paint on it. Find out who that dress belongs to. Find out how the person can account for having been in the room, and smeared the paint between midnight and three in the morning. If the person can't satisfy you, you haven't far to look for the hand that took the Diamond."

One after another those words travelled over my memory, repeating themselves again and again with a wearisome, mechanical reiteration. I was roused from what felt like a trance of many hours – from what was really, no doubt, the pause of a few moments only – by a voice calling to me. I looked up, and saw that Betteredge's patience had failed him at last. He was just visible between the sand hills, returning to the beach.

The old man's appearance recalled me, the moment I perceived it, to my sense of present things, and reminded me that the inquiry which I had pursued thus far, still remained incomplete. I had discovered the smear on the nightgown. To whom did the nightgown belong?

My first impulse was to consult the letter in my pocket – the letter which I had found in the case.

As I raised my hand to take it out, I remembered that there was a shorter way to discovery than this. The nightgown itself would reveal the truth; for, in all probability, the nightgown was marked with its owner's name.

I took it up from the sand, and looked for the mark.

I found the mark, and read –

MY OWN NAME.

There were the familiar letters which told me that the nightgown was mine. I looked up from them. There was the sun; there were the glittering waters of the bay; there was old Betteredge, advancing nearer and nearer to me. I looked back again at the letters. My own name. Plainly confronting me – my own name.

"If time, pains, and money can do it, I will lay my hand on the thief who took the Moonstone." – I had left London, with those words on my lips. I had penetrated the secret which the quicksand had kept from every other living creature. And, on the unanswerable evidence of the paint-stain, I had discovered Myself as the Thief.

Drawing a Blank
Arthur W Pinero, 1905

The first act of English dramatist Arthur Pinero's (1855–1934) play *In Chancery* takes place in the parlour of the Railway Hotel, where Montague Joliffe and his doctor debate the trials and benefits of memory loss.

JOL. (*solemnly*) Dr Titus, you remember my being brought to the Railway Inn at Steepleton, don't you?

TITUS. Of course I do, six weeks ago.

JOL. Six weeks at Steepleton Junction. (*turning and pointing*) You can see the exact spot from that window. Two passenger trains came into violent collision. *Nothing resulted* but a few scratches and bruises and everybody was able after a *trifling delay* to resume their journey, everybody with *one* important *exception*.

TITUS. Yourself.

JOL. (*myself.*) I was carefully deposited in the best bedroom of the Railway Hotel, where, owing to the assiduous nursing of that kind creature there, (*pointing to* PAT.) and the unremitting attention of Dr Titus, (*taking* TITUS's *hand*) in three weeks I was on my legs again.

TITUS. As strong as a horse.

AMNESIA

JOL. Strong as a tandem, never *was* better, at least I don't think I ever was better, but Dr Titus, I don't remember.

TITUS. Don't remember?

JOL. No, I'm vigorous and hearty, can eat, drink and sleep, I'm well educated, can speak French, jabber a little German, know a phrase or two of Italian, and have a fair knowledge of music, but, Dr Titus, ever since that little smash up at Steepleton Junction, I haven't the least idea who the devil I am, whence I came, or where I'm going.

TITUS. Good gracious, what's wrong?

(*Music stops*)

JOL. My memory! My mind's a perfect blank as to the past, every incident of, I hope, my distinguished career previous to that railway accident has entirely left me.

TITUS. But you know your name.

JOL. (*producing card-case*) Yes, but only thro' finding my card-case in my overcoat pocket. (*handing card to* TITUS.)

JOL. Here it is, Montague Joliffe, no address. MJ, No.36 was marked on my collars, which leads me to hope I am a gentleman.

TITUS. Why?

JOL. Well, nobody but a gentleman would have 36 white three-fold linen masher collars.

TITUS. Well, this is another most interesting case! Have you searched all the directories?

JOL. (*with a look of horror*) No!

TITUS. Why not?

JOL. I'm afraid to.

TITUS. Nonsense! Do it at once. (*rises*)

JOL. No, no, no! I might turn out to be a party I don't like. I might have to follow a trade or profession I detest, or what is more awful, I might discover my profession without remembering how to practice it. I might find myself a colonel, who has forgotten his drill, a captain in the navy who knows nothing but how to be sea-sick, or a doctor who cannot remember the pharmacopoeia. In short, I may be a soldier, sailor, apothecary, ploughboy or a thief.

TITUS. Ah, but on the other hand!

JOL. On the other hand, I may be the hero of the hour, the author of the latest craze in books, the new drawing-room tenor, or the fashionable tragedian. I may be an MP, one of the Cabinet, or perhaps a member of the County Court. It's this that buoys me up. But Dr Titus, I shan't be able to stand the uncertainty much longer. Give me your opinion. (*he rises and puts himself in studied position*) Now, what do you think I am?

TITUS. (*sitting, leaning back and surveying him*) A very lucky fellow.

JOL. Lucky?

TITUS. Certainly, why, it's as much as I can do to forget a few tradesmen's bills. You want my advice?

JOL. Yes.

TITUS. Take it easy; accept your position. You'll never have so little anxiety as you have at the present moment. How old are you?

JOL. Don't know. What do you think? (*anxiously*) Think I'm a chicken?

TITUS. Well, you're in the prime of life, with no conscience to prick you on the score of past misdeeds, enjoy yourself, make merry, until your recollections return. (*rises, bus. chair*)

JOL. Oh, they will return then?

TITUS. Of course they will, all of a sudden, your case is no rarer in the annals of medicine than it is in fiction. When those two railway engines came together you experienced a shock?

JOL. I did.

TITUS. *That's the cause.*

(*Music as before*)

One day without a moment's warning, like the bursting of a soap bubble in a man's ear, your memory will come back to you. The sight of somebody's ugly face, the sound of a familiar voice, the melody of a miserable comic song, or the air of a waltz from a discordant organ, and the rusty gates of the past will be opened. Like a flash of lightning you will regain the consciousness of cares and responsibilities, arrears of income-tax unpaid, and all the evils of a well-spent life. Be warned, don't seek to hasten matters, and in the meantime be happy.

(*Music ceases*)

Feather Brain
Sarah Grice, 2012

Common terms like 'featherbrain' and 'absent minded' depict forgetfulness as a physical affliction of the entire brain. In both phrases the organ appears to lack substance, or even to have floated away.

'The Uncapturable Whirling Medley'
Marcel Proust, 1913

C K Scott Moncrieff lifted a line from a Shakespeare
sonnet to title his English translation of Marcel Proust's
(1871–1922) *À la Recherche du Temps Perdu*. However,
'remembrance of things past' misrepresents the central
theme of the multi-volume novel, which is more accurately
a celebration of involuntary memory. This extract is taken
from the overture to the first volume, *Swann's Way*.

And so it is with our own past. It is a labour in vain to attempt
to recapture it: all the efforts of our intellect must prove futile.
The past is hidden somewhere outside the realm, beyond
the reach of intellect, in some material object (in the sensation which that material object will give us) which we do not
suspect. And as for that object, it depends on chance whether
we come upon it or not before we ourselves must die.

Many years had elapsed during which nothing of Combray,
save what was comprised in the theatre and the drama of
my going to bed there, had any existence for me, when one
day in winter, as I came home, my mother, seeing that I was
cold, offered me some tea, a thing I did not ordinarily take. I
declined at first, and then, for no particular reason, changed
my mind. She sent out for one of those short, plump little
cakes called 'petites madeleines,' which look as though they
had been moulded in the fluted scallop of a pilgrim's shell.
And soon, mechanically, weary after a dull day with the
prospect of a depressing morrow, I raised to my lips a spoonful
of the tea in which I had soaked a morsel of the cake. No
sooner had the warm liquid, and the crumbs with it, touched
my palate than a shudder ran through my whole body, and
I stopped, intent upon the extraordinary changes that were
taking place. An exquisite pleasure had invaded my senses, but

individual, detached, with no suggestion of its origin. And at once the vicissitudes of life had become indifferent to me, its disasters innocuous, its brevity illusory – this new sensation having had on me the effect which love has of filling me with a precious essence; or rather this essence was not in me, it was myself. I had ceased now to feel mediocre, accidental, mortal. Whence could it have come to me, this all-powerful joy? I was conscious that it was connected with the taste of tea and cake, but that it infinitely transcended those savours, could not, indeed, be of the same nature as theirs. Whence did it come? What did it signify? How could I seize upon and define it?

I drink a second mouthful, in which I find nothing more than in the first, a third, which gives me rather less than the second. It is time to stop; the potion is losing its magic. It is plain that the object of my quest, the truth, lies not in the cup but in myself. The tea has called up in me, but does not itself understand, and can only repeat indefinitely with a gradual loss of strength, the same testimony; which I, too, cannot interpret, though I hope at least to be able to call upon the tea for it again and to find it there presently, intact and at my disposal, for my final enlightenment. I put down my cup and examine my own mind. It is for it to discover the truth. But how? What an abyss of uncertainty whenever the mind feels that some part of it has strayed beyond its own borders; when it, the seeker, is at once the dark region through which it must go seeking, where all its equipment will avail it nothing. Seek? More than that: create. It is face to face with something which does not so far exist, to which it alone can give reality and substance, which it alone can bring into the light of day.

And I begin again to ask myself what it could have been, this unremembered state which brought with it no logical proof of its existence, but only the sense that it was a happy, that it was a real state in whose presence other states of consciousness melted and vanished. I decide to attempt

to make it reappear. I retrace my thoughts to the moment
at which I drank the first spoonful of tea. I find again the
same state, illumined by no fresh light. I compel my mind to
make one further effort, to follow and recapture once again
the fleeting sensation. And that nothing may interrupt it in
its course I shut out every obstacle, every extraneous idea,
I stop my ears and inhibit all attention to the sounds which
come from the next room. And then, feeling that my mind
is growing fatigued without having any success to report, I
compel it for a change to enjoy that distraction which I have
just denied it, to think of other things, to rest and refresh itself
before the supreme attempt. And then for the second time I
clear an empty space in front of it. I place in position before my
mind's eye the still recent taste of that first mouthful, and I feel
something start within me, something that leaves its resting-
place and attempts to rise, something that has been embedded
like an anchor at a great depth; I do not know yet what it is, but
I can feel it mounting slowly; I can measure the resistance, I
can hear the echo of great spaces traversed.

Undoubtedly what is thus palpitating in the depths of my
being must be the image, the visual memory which, being
linked to that taste, has tried to follow it into my conscious
mind. But its struggles are too far off, too much confused;
scarcely can I perceive the colourless reflection in which are
blended the uncapturable whirling medley of radiant hues,
and I cannot distinguish its form, cannot invite it, as the
one possible interpreter, to translate to me the evidence of
its contemporary, its inseparable paramour, the taste of cake
soaked in tea; cannot ask it to inform me what special circumstance is in question, of what period in my past life.

Will it ultimately reach the clear surface of my consciousness, this memory, this old, dead moment which the magnetism of an identical moment has travelled so far to importune,
to disturb, to raise up out of the very depths of my being? I

cannot tell. Now that I feel nothing, it has stopped, has perhaps gone down again into its darkness, from which who can say whether it will ever rise? Ten times over I must essay the task, must lean down over the abyss. And each time the natural laziness which deters us from every difficult enterprise, every work of importance, has urged me to leave the thing alone, to drink my tea and to think merely of the worries of to-day and of my hopes for to-morrow, which let themselves be pondered over without effort or distress of mind.

And suddenly the memory returns. The taste was that of the little crumb of madeleine which on Sunday mornings at Combray (because on those mornings I did not go out before church-time), when I went to say good day to her in her bedroom, my aunt Léonie used to give me, dipping it first in her own cup of real or of lime-flower tea. The sight of the little madeleine had recalled nothing to my mind before I tasted it; perhaps because I had so often seen such things in the interval, without tasting them, on the trays in pastry-cooks' windows, that their image had dissociated itself from those Combray days to take its place among others more recent; perhaps because of those memories, so long abandoned and put out of mind, nothing now survived, everything was scattered; the forms of things, including that of the little scallop-shell of pastry, so richly sensual under its severe, religious folds, were either obliterated or had been so long dormant as to have lost the power of expansion which would have allowed them to resume their place in my consciousness. But when from a long-distant past nothing subsists, after the people are dead, after the things are broken and scattered, still, alone, more fragile, but with more vitality, more unsubstantial, more persistent, more faithful, the smell and taste of things remain poised a long time, like souls, ready to remind us, waiting and hoping for their moment, amid the ruins of all the rest; and bear unfaltering, in the tiny and almost impalpable drop of their essence, the vast structure of recollection.

And once I had recognised the taste of the crumb of madeleine soaked in her decoction of lime-flowers which my aunt used to give me (although I did not yet know and must long postpone the discovery of why this memory made me so happy) immediately the old grey house upon the street, where her room was, rose up like the scenery of a theatre to attach itself to the little pavilion, opening on to the garden, which had been built out behind it for my parents (the isolated panel which until that moment had been all that I could see); and with the house the town, from morning to night and in all weathers, the Square where I was sent before luncheon, the streets along which I used to run errands, the country roads we took when it was fine. And just as the Japanese amuse themselves by filling a porcelain bowl with water and steeping in it little crumbs of paper which until then are without character or form, but, the moment they become wet, stretch themselves and bend, take on colour and distinctive shape, become flowers or houses or people, permanent and recognisable, so in that moment all the flowers in our garden and in M. Swann's park, and the water-lilies on the Vivonne and the good folk of the village and their little dwellings and the parish church and the whole of Combray and of its surroundings, taking their proper shapes and growing solid, sprang into being, town and gardens alike, from my cup of tea.

Memory Theatre
Robert Fludd, 1619

English physician Robert Fludd's (1574–1637) theatrical stage provides a structure for storing memories. Placing images and objects beside specific points, like the doors and pillar bases, is intended to aid recall.

The Mind of a Mnemonist
Alexander Luria, 1968

> Russian psychologist Alexander Luria (1902–1977) spent
> several decades studying Solomon Shereshevsky (known
> as S), whose power of recall was so strong he worked as a
> professional memory man. In this extract from *The Mind of
> a Mnemonist* Luria explores the impact of S's synaesthesia.

What this indicates is that for S there was no distinct line,
as there is for others of us, separating vision from hearing,
or hearing from a sense of touch or taste. The remnants of
synaesthesia that many ordinary people have, which are of a
very rudimentary sort (experiencing lower and higher tones
as having different colourations; regarding some tones as
'warm,' others as 'cold'; 'seeing' Friday and Monday as having
different colours), were central to S's psychic life. These
synaesthetic experiences not only appeared very early in his life
but persisted right to his death. And, as we shall have occasion
to see, they left their mark on his habits of perception, understanding, and thought, and were a vital feature of his memory.

S's tendency to recall material in terms of 'lines' or
'splashes' came into play whenever he had to deal with isolated
sounds, nonsense syllables, or words he was not familiar with.
He pointed out that in these circumstances sounds, voices,
or words evoked some visual impression such as 'puffs of
steam,' 'splashes,' 'smooth or broken lines'; sometimes they
also produced a sensation of taste, at other times a sensation
of touch, of his having come into contact with something he
would describe as 'prickly,' 'smooth,' or 'rough.'

These synaesthetic components of each visual and particularly of each auditory stimulus had been an inherent part of
S's recall at a very early age; it was only later, after his faculty
for logical and figurative memory had developed, that these

tended to fade into the background, though they continued to play some part in his recall.

From an objective standpoint these synaesthetic components were important to his recall, for they created, as it were, a background for each recollection, furnishing him with additional, 'extra' information that would guarantee accurate recall. If, as we shall see later, S was prompted to reproduce a word inaccurately, the additional synaesthetic sensations he experienced would fail to coincide with the word he produced, leaving him with the sense that something was wrong with his response and forcing him to correct the error.

> ...*I recognise a word not only by the images it evokes but by a whole complex of feelings that image arouses. It's hard to express... it's not a matter of vision or hearing but some overall sense I get. Usually I experience a word's taste and weight, and I don't have to make an effort to remember it – the word seems to recall itself. But it's difficult to describe. What I sense is something oily slipping through my hand... or I'm aware of a slight tickling in my left hand caused by a mass of tiny, lightweight points. When that happens I simply remember, without having to make the attempt...*

Record of May 22, 1939

How Reliable Is Your Memory?
Elizabeth Loftus, 2013

> American psychologist Elizabeth Loftus (b. 1944) closed her
> TEDGlobal talk on the reliability of memory with a request
> to accept memory as a fragile thing. This extract offers a
> worrying example of the difficulty of distinguishing between
> true and false memories.

I'd like to tell you about a legal case that I worked on involving
a man named Steve Titus.

Titus was a restaurant manager. He was 31 years old,
he lived in Seattle, Washington, he was engaged to Gretchen,
about to be married, she was the love of his life. And
one night, the couple went out for a romantic restaurant
meal. They were on their way home, and they were pulled over
by a police officer. You see, Titus's car sort of resembled a car
that was driven earlier in the evening by a man who raped a
female hitchhiker, and Titus kind of resembled that rapist. So
the police took a picture of Titus, they put it in a photo
line-up, they later showed it to the victim, and she pointed to
Titus's photo. She said, "That one's the closest." The police
and the prosecution proceeded with a trial, and when Steve
Titus was put on trial for rape, the rape victim got on the
stand and said, "I'm absolutely positive that's the man." And
Titus was convicted. He proclaimed his innocence, his
family screamed at the jury, his fiancée collapsed on the floor
sobbing, and Titus is taken away to jail.

So what would you do at this point? What would you
do? Well, Titus lost complete faith in the legal system, and
yet he got an idea. He called up the local newspaper, he got
the interest of an investigative journalist, and that journalist
actually found the real rapist, a man who ultimately confessed
to this rape, a man who was thought to have committed fifty

FALSE MEMORIES | MEMORY CONSTRUCTION

rapes in that area, and when this information was given to the judge, the judge set Titus free.

And really, that's where this case should have ended. It should have been over. Titus should have thought of this as a horrible year, a year of accusation and trial, but over.

It didn't end that way. Titus was so bitter. He'd lost his job. He couldn't get it back. He lost his fiancée. She couldn't put up with his persistent anger. He lost his entire savings, and so he decided to file a lawsuit against the police and others whom he felt were responsible for his suffering.

And that's when I really started working on this case, trying to figure out how did that victim go from "That one's the closest" to "I'm absolutely positive that's the guy."

Well, Titus was consumed with his civil case. He spent every waking moment thinking about it, and just days before he was to have his day in court, he woke up in the morning, doubled over in pain, and died of a stress-related heart attack. He was 35 years old.

So I was asked to work on Titus's case because I'm a psychological scientist. I study memory. I've studied memory for decades. And if I meet somebody on an airplane – this happened on the way over to Scotland – if I meet somebody on an airplane, and we ask each other, "What do you do? What do you do?" and I say "I study memory," they usually want to tell me how they have trouble remembering names, or they've got a relative who's got Alzheimer's or some kind of memory problem, but I have to tell them I don't study when people forget. I study the opposite: when they remember, when they remember things that didn't happen or remember things that were different from the way they really were. I study false memories.

Unhappily, Steve Titus is not the only person to be convicted based on somebody's false memory. In one project in the United States, information has been gathered on 300 innocent people, 300 defendants who were convicted of crimes they didn't do. They spent 10, 20, 30 years in prison for these crimes, and now DNA testing has proven that they are actually innocent. And when those cases have been analysed, three quarters of them are due to faulty memory, faulty eyewitness memory.

Well, why? Like the jurors who convicted those innocent people and the jurors who convicted Titus, many people believe that memory works like a recording device. You just record the information, then you call it up and play it back when you want to answer questions or identify images. But decades of work in psychology has shown that this just isn't true. Our memories are constructive. They're reconstructive. Memory works a little bit more like a Wikipedia page: You can go in there and change it, but so can other people. I first started studying this constructive memory process in the 1970s. I did my experiments that involved showing people simulated crimes and accidents and asking them questions about what they remember. In one study, we showed people a simulated accident and we asked people, how fast were the cars going when they hit each other? And we asked other people, how fast were the cars going when they smashed into each other? And if we asked the leading "smashed" question, the witnesses told us the cars were going faster, and moreover, that leading "smashed" question caused people to be more likely to tell us that they saw broken glass in the accident scene when there wasn't any broken glass at all. In another study, we showed a simulated accident where a car went through an intersection with a stop sign, and if we asked a question that insinuated it was a yield sign, many witnesses told us they remember seeing a yield sign at the intersection, not a stop sign.

And you might be thinking, well, you know, these are filmed events, they are not particularly stressful. Would the same kind of mistakes be made with a really stressful event? In a study we published just a few months ago, we have an answer to this question, because what was unusual about this study is we arranged for people to have a very stressful experience. The subjects in this study were members of the US military who were undergoing a harrowing training exercise to teach them what it's going to be like for them if they are ever captured as prisoners of war. And as part of this training exercise, these soldiers are interrogated in an aggressive, hostile, physically abusive fashion for 30 minutes and later on they have to try to identify the person who conducted that interrogation. And when we feed them suggestive information that insinuates it's a different person, many of them misidentify their interrogator, often identifying someone who doesn't even remotely resemble the real interrogator.

And so what these studies are showing is that when you feed people misinformation about some experience that they may have had, you can distort or contaminate or change their memory.

Well out there in the real world, misinformation is everywhere. We get misinformation not only if we're questioned in a leading way, but if we talk to other witnesses who might consciously or inadvertently feed us some erroneous information, or if we see media coverage about some event we might have experienced, all of these provide the opportunity for this kind of contamination of our memory.

'Retroactive Hallucinations'
Hippolyte Bernheim, 1889

> French physician Hippolyte Bernheim (1840–1919)
> considered states of consciousness to be infinitely
> varying. This disturbing hypnotic intervention, published
> in *Suggestive Therapeutics*, may be the first documented
> example of an implanted trauma memory.

...I have proved that true *retroactive hallucinations* may often
be developed. We can suggest to subjects that at some period,
now past, they saw such and such an act committed, and the
image created in their minds seems like a living memory,
which governs them to such an extent as to appear an incon-
testable reality.

For example, here is the case of a somnambulist, Marie
G—, an intelligent woman of whom I have already spoken,
I hypnotise her into deep sleep and say, "You got up in the
night?" She replies, "Oh, no." "I insist upon it; you got up four
times to go to the water-closet, and the fourth time you fell on
your nose. This is a fact, and when you wake up no one will be
able to make you believe the contrary." When she wakes I ask,
"How are you now?" "Very well," she answers, "but last night I
had an attack of diarrhoea. I had to get up four times. I fell too,
and hurt my nose." I say, "You dreamed that. You said nothing
to me about it just now. Not one of the patients saw you."
She persists in her statement, saying that she has not been
dreaming, that she was perfectly conscious of getting up, that
all the patients were asleep; – and she remains convinced that
the occurrence was genuine.

On another occasion, while she was sleeping, I asked
what house she lived in, and who else lived there. Among
other things, she told me that the first floor was occupied by
a family, – mother, father, and several little girls, and an old

IMPLANTED MEMORIES | HYPNOSIS

bachelor who lived with them. Then I gave her the following
suggestion: "On August 3 (three months and a half ago), at
three o'clock in the afternoon, you went into the house where
you live. When you reached the first floor, you heard cries
coming from a room. You looked in through the key-hole.
You saw the old bachelor committing rape upon the largest
little girl: you saw it. The little girl was struggling, she was
bleeding, and he gagged her. You saw it all, and you were so
distressed that you went to your apartment and did not dare
to say anything. When you wake up you will think no more
about it. I have not told the story to you; it is not a dream; it is
not a vision I have given you during your hypnotic sleep; it is
truth itself; and if inquiry is made into this crime later on, you
will tell the truth." I then changed the course of her ideas, and
gave her brighter suggestions. When she woke, I did not dare
to speak of the fact. I asked my friend M. Grillon, a distinguished lawyer, to question the woman three days later, as if
he were a judge deputed to do so. She related the facts to him
in my absence, giving all the details, the names of the criminal
and the victim, and the exact hour of the crime. She gave her
evidence energetically. She knew the gravity of her testimony.
If she was summoned before the assizes, she would tell the
truth in spite of her feelings. If it were necessary, she was ready
to swear before God and man! As I approached her bed after
her evidence was given, the lawyer, assuming the privilege
of a magistrate, made her repeat the evidence before me. I
asked her if it was really true; if she had not been dreaming;
if it was not a vision like those I was in the habit of giving
her during her sleep. I tried to persuade her to doubt herself.
She maintained the truth of her testimony with immovable
conviction.

After that I hypnotised her in order to take away this
suggestion. "Everything you told the judge was a mistake," I
said, "you saw nothing on August 3. You know nothing about

anything of the kind. You will not even remember that you have spoken to the judge. He has asked no questions and you have told him nothing." When she waked I said to her, "What did you say to M— just now?" – "I said nothing" – "What, you said nothing!" replied the magistrate. "You told me about a crime which occurred on August 3, in the house where you live. You saw the person named X— , etc."

Marie was disconcerted. The news of the crime took away her breath. She had never heard of it. When M— insisted, telling her that she herself had mentioned this crime, she could not understand. She was violently affected by the news that she would be summoned to court as a witness, and to calm her I had to hypnotise her again and wipe out the memory of this truly frightful scene. When she woke again, the memory of all that had passed was effectually erased from her mind, and the next day when talking with her, I purposely led her to speak of the people in the house where she lived. She spoke of them naturally, as if we had never mentioned them when together.

False Memory Archive: Erased UFOs
A R Hopwood, 2012–14

Artist A R Hopwood collaborates with experts and the public to explore the nature, consequences and meaning of false memories. In this installation Hopwood presents 242 found photographs of UFO sightings, in which all evidence of alien objects has been digitally erased.

4: Being | Not Being

Simulating death | *Signs of life* |
Suspended animation | *The living
dead* | Zombies | *Paralysis* | Locked-in
syndrome | *Unawareness* | Prolonged
unconsciousness | *Persistent vegetative
state* | Minimal consciousness |
Anaesthesia | Awareness | *Life support*
| Unconsciousness | *Premature burial*
| Confirmation of death | *Dying* | Life
after death | *Heightened consciousness*
| Rebirth | *Resurrection* | Galvanism |
Personal consciousness | Brain–machine
interfacing

Playing Dead
Andrew Hudgins, 2005

The playful protagonist of these verses by American poet
Andrew Hudgins (b. 1951) makes a convincing corpse until
one of his children implements a painfully effective dead-
or-alive test.

> Our father liked to play a game.
> He played that he was dead.
> He took his thick black glasses off
> and stretched out on the bed.
>
> He wouldn't twitch and didn't snore
> or move in any way.
> He didn't even seem to breathe!
> We asked, *Are you okay?*
>
> We tickled fingers up and down
> his huge, pink, stinky feet –
> He didn't move; he lay as still
> as last year's parakeet.
>
> We pushed our fingers up his nose,
> and wiggled them inside –
> Next, we peeled his eyelids back.
> *Are you okay?* we cried.
>
> I really thought he might be dead
> and not just playing possum,
> because his eyeballs didn't twitch
> when I slid my tongue across 'em.

SIMULATING DEATH | SIGNS OF LIFE

He's dead, we sobbed – but to be sure,
I jabbed him in the jewels.
He rose, like Jesus, from the dead,
though I don't think Jesus drools.

His right hand lashed both right and left.
His left hand clutched his scrotum.
And the words he yelled – I know damn well
I'm way too young to quote 'em.

Sarah Bernhardt Asleep in Her Coffin
Unknown artist, *c.*1882

French actress Sarah Bernhardt (1844–1923) acquired a
coffin as a teenager and is said to have slept in the satin-
lined casket. Many people assumed this portrait, which
mimics post-mortem photography of the time, showed
Bernhardt's corpse. In fact, she lived another 40 years.

'This Borrow'd Likeness of Shrunk Death'
William Shakespeare, 1597

In William Shakespeare's (1564–1616) *Romeo and Juliet*
Friar Laurence helps Juliet "undertake a thing like death".

Take thou this phial, being then in bed,
And this distilled liquor drink thou off:
When, presently, through all thy veins shall run
A cold and drowsy humour, which shall seize
Each vital spirit; for no pulse shall keep
His natural progress, but surcease to beat:
No warmth, no breath, shall testify thou liv'st;
The roses in thy lips and cheeks shall fade
To paly ashes; thy eyes' windows fall,
Like death, when he shuts up the day of life;
Each part, depriv'd of supple government,
Shall, stiff and stark, and cold, appear like death:
And in this borrow'd likeness of shrunk death
Thou shalt remain full two and forty hours,
And then awake as from a pleasant sleep.
Now when the bridegroom in the morning comes
To rouse thee from thy bed, there art thou dead:
Then (as the manner of our country is,)
In thy best robes uncover'd on the bier,
Thou shalt be borne to that same ancient vault,
Where all the kindred of the Capulets lie.
In the mean time, against thou shalt awake,
Shall Romeo by my letters know our drift;
And hither shall he come; and he and I
Will watch thy waking, and that very night
Shall Romeo bear thee hence to Mantua.

SIMULATING DEATH | SUSPENDED ANIMATION

Dead Men Working in the Cane Fields
W B Seabrook, 1929

> American journalist William Buehler Seabrook's (1884–
> 1945) Haitian travelogue *Magic Island* introduced 'walking
> dead men', or 'zombies', to English-language readers.

My first impression of the three supposed *zombies*, who
continued dumbly at work, was that there was something
about them unnatural and strange. They were plodding like
brutes, like automatons. Without stooping down, I could not
fully see their faces, which were bent expressionless over their
work. Polynice touched one of them on the shoulder, motioned
him to get up. Obediently, like an animal, he slowly stood erect
– and what I saw then, coupled with what I had heard previously, or despite it, came as a rather sickening shock. The eyes
were the worst. It was not my imagination. They were in truth
like the eyes of a dead man, not blind, but staring, unfocused,
unseeing. The whole face, for that matter, was bad enough. It
was vacant, as if there was nothing behind it. It seemed not
only expressionless, but incapable of expression. I had seen
so much previously in Haiti that was outside ordinary normal
experience that for the flash of a second I had a sickening,
almost panicky lapse in which I thought, or rather felt, "Great
God, maybe this stuff is really true, and if it is true, it is rather
awful, for it upsets everything." By "everything" I meant the
natural fixed laws and processes on which all modern human
thought and actions are based. Then suddenly I remembered
– and my mind seized the memory as a man sinking in water
clutches a solid plank – the face of a dog I had once seen in the
histological laboratory at Columbia. Its entire front brain had
been removed in an experimental operation weeks before; it
moved about, it was alive, but its eyes were like the eyes I now
saw staring.

I recovered from my mental panic. I reached out and grasped one of the dangling hands. It was calloused, solid, human. Holding it, I said, *"Bonjour, compare."* The zombie stared without responding.

'Who Knows What She May Be Thinking?'
Émile Zola, 1867

In French writer Émile Zola's (1840–1902) novel *Thérèse Raquin* the titular character's aunt is paralysed and struck dumb after her son Camille disappears.

The crisis threatening Madame Raquin took place. The paralysis, which for several months had been creeping along her limbs, always ready to strangle her, at last took her by the throat and linked her body. One evening, while conversing peacefully with Thérèse and Laurent, she remained in the middle of a sentence with her mouth wide open: she felt as if she was being throttled. When she wanted to cry out and call for help, she could only splutter a few hoarse sounds. Her hands and feet were rigid. She found herself struck dumb, and powerless to move.

Thérèse and Laurent rose from their chairs, terrified at this stroke, which had contorted the old mercer in less than five seconds. When she became rigid, and fixed her suplicating eyes on them, they pressed her with questions in order to ascertain the cause of her suffering. Unable to reply, she continued gazing at them in profound anguish.

They then understood that they had nothing but a corpse before them, a corpse half alive that could see and hear, but could not speak to them. They were in despair at this attack. At the bottom of their hearts, they cared little for the suffering of the paralysed woman. They mourned over themselves, who in future would have to live alone, face to face.

From this day the life of the married couple became intolerable. They passed the most cruel evenings opposite the impotent old lady, who no longer lulled their terror with her gentle, idle talk. She reposed in an armchair, like a parcel, a thing, while they remained alone, one at each end of the table, embarrassed and anxious. This body no longer separated them; at times they forgot it, confounding it with the articles of furniture.

They were now seized with the same terror as at night. The dining-room became, like the bedroom, a terrible spot, where the spectre of Camille arose, causing them to suffer an extra four or five hours daily. As soon as twilight came, they shuddered, lowering the lamp-shade so as not to see one another, and endeavouring to persuade themselves that Madame Raquin was about to speak and thus remind them of her presence. If they kept her with them, if they did not get rid of her, it was because her eyes were still alive, and they experienced a little relief in watching them move and sparkle.

They always placed the impotent old lady in the bright beam of the lamp, so as to thoroughly light up her face and have it always before them. This flabby, livid countenance would have been a sight that others could not have borne, but Thérèse and Laurent experienced such need for company, that they gazed upon it with real joy.

This face looked like that of a dead person in the centre of which two living eyes had been fixed. These eyes alone moved, rolling rapidly in their orbits. The cheeks and mouth maintained such appalling immobility that they seemed as though petrified. When Madame Raquin fell asleep and lowered her lids, her countenance, which was then quite white and mute, was really that of a corpse. Thérèse and Laurent, who no longer felt anyone with them, then made a noise until the paralysed woman raised her eyelids and looked at them.

In this manner they compelled her to remain awake.

They regarded her as a distraction that drew them from their bad dreams. Since she had been infirm, they had to attend to her like a child. The care they lavished on her forced them to scatter their thoughts. In the morning Laurent lifted her up and bore her to her armchair; at night he placed her on her bed again. She was still heavy, and he had to exert all his strength to raise her delicately in his arms, and carry her. It was also he who rolled her armchair along. The other attentions fell to Thérèse. She dressed and fed the impotent old lady, and sought to understand her slightest wish.

For a few days Madame Raquin preserved the use of her hands. She could write on a slate, and in this way asked for what she required; then the hands withered, and it became impossible for her to raise them or hold a pencil. From that moment her eyes were her only language, and it was necessary for her niece to guess what she desired. The young woman devoted herself to the hard duties of sick-nurse, which gave her occupation for body and mind that did her much good.

So as not to remain face to face, the married couple rolled the armchair of the poor old lady into the dining-room, the first thing in the morning. They placed her between them, as if she were necessary to their existence. They caused her to be present at their meals, and at all their interviews. When she signified the desire to retire to her bedroom, they feigned not to understand. She was only of use to interrupt their private conversations, and had no right to live apart.

At eight o'clock, Laurent went to his studio, Thérèse descended to the shop, while the paralysed woman remained alone in the dining-room until noon; then, after lunch, she found herself without company again until six o'clock. Frequently, during the day, her niece ran upstairs, and, hovering round her, made sure she did not require anything. The friends of the family were at a loss for sufficiently laudatory phrases wherein to extol the virtues of Thérèse and Laurent.

The Thursday receptions continued, the impotent old lady being present, as in the past. Her armchair was advanced to the table, and from eight o'clock till eleven she kept her eyes open, casting penetrating glances from one to another of her guests in turn. On the first few of these evenings, old Michaud and Grivet felt some embarrassment in the presence of the corpse of their old friend. They did not know what countenance to put on. They only experienced moderate sorrow, and they were inquiring in their minds in what measure it would be suitable to display their grief. Should they speak to this lifeless face? Should they refrain from troubling about it? Little by little, they decided to treat Madame Raquin as though nothing had happened to her. They ended by feigning to completely ignore her condition. They chatted with her, putting questions and giving the answers, laughing both for her and for themselves, and never permitting the rigid expression on the countenance to baffle them.

It was a strange sight: these men who appeared to be speaking sensibly to a statue, just as little girls talk to their dolls. The paralysed woman sat rigid and mute before them, while they babbled, multiplying their gestures in exceedingly animated conversations with her. Michaud and Grivet prided themselves on their correct attitude. In acting as they did, they believed they were giving proof of politeness; they, moreover, avoided the annoyance of the customary condolences. They fancied that Madame Raquin must feel flattered to find herself treated as a person in good health; and, from that moment, it became possible for them to be merry in her presence, without the least scruple.

Grivet had contracted a mania. He affirmed that Madame Raquin and himself understood one another perfectly; and that she could not look at him without him at once comprehending what she desired. This was another delicate attention. Only Grivet was on every occasion in error. He frequently interrupted the game of dominoes, to observe the infirm woman whose eyes were quietly following the game, and declare that she wanted such or such a thing. On further inquiry it was found that she wanted nothing at all, or that she wanted something entirely different. This did not discourage Grivet, who triumphantly exclaimed:

"Just as I said!" And he began again a few moments later.

It was quite another matter when the impotent old lady openly expressed a desire; Thérèse, Laurent, and the guests named one object after another that they fancied she might wish for. Grivet then made himself remarkable by the clumsiness of his offers. He mentioned, haphazard, everything that came into his head, invariably offering the contrary to what Madame Raquin desired. But this circumstance did not prevent him repeating:

"I can read in her eyes as in a book. Look, she says I am right. Is it not so, dear lady? Yes, yes."

Nevertheless, it was no easy matter to grasp the wishes of the poor old woman. Thérèse alone possessed this faculty. She communicated fairly well with this walled-up brain, still alive, but buried in a lifeless frame. What was passing within this wretched creature, just sufficiently alive to be present at the events of life, without taking part in them? She saw and heard, she no doubt reasoned in a distinct and clear manner. But she was without gesture and voice to express the thoughts originating in her mind. Her ideas were perhaps choking her, and yet she could not raise a hand, nor open her mouth, even though one of her movements or words should decide the destiny of the world.

Her mind resembled those of the living buried by mistake, who awaken in the middle of the night in the earth, three or four yards below the surface of the ground. They shout, they struggle, and people pass over them without hearing their atrocious lamentations.

Laurent frequently gazed at Madame Raquin, his lips pressed together, his hands stretched out on his knees, putting all his life into his sparkling and swiftly moving eyes. And he said to himself:

"Who knows what she may be thinking of all alone? Some cruel drama must be passing within this inanimate frame."

Laurent made a mistake. Madame Raquin was happy, happy at the care and affection bestowed on her by her dear children. She had always dreamed of ending in this gentle way, amidst devotedness and caresses. Certainly she would have been pleased to have preserved her speech, so as to be able to thank the friends who assisted her to die in peace. But she accepted her condition without rebellion. The tranquil and retired life she had always led, the sweetness of her character, prevented her feeling too acutely the suffering of being mute and unable to make a movement. She had entered second childhood. She passed days without weariness, gazing before her, and musing on the past. She even tasted the charm of remaining very good in her armchair, like a little girl.

Each day the sweetness and brightness of her eyes became more penetrating. She had reached the point of making them perform the duties of a hand or mouth, in asking for what she required and in expressing her thanks. In this way she replaced the organs that were wanting, in a most peculiar and charming manner. Her eyes, in the centre of her flabby and grimacing face, were of celestial beauty.

Since her twisted and inert lips could no longer smile, she smiled with adorable tenderness, by her looks; moist beams and rays of dawn issued from her orbits. Nothing was more peculiar than those eyes which laughed like lips in this lifeless countenance. The lower part of the face remained gloomy and wan, while the upper part was divinely lit up. It was particularly for her beloved children that she placed all her gratitude, all the affection of her soul into a simple glance. When Laurent took her in his arms, morning and night, to carry her, she thanked him lovingly by looks full of tender effusion.

Medical Aspects of the Persistent Vegetative State
The Multi-Society Task Force on PVS, 1994

Ever since the term 'persistent vegetative state' (PVS) emerged in 1972, it has been paired with ethical and legal debates about withholding or withdrawing medical treatment. In 1991 a multi-society task force was formed to gather the medical facts about PVS. This abstract summarises the group's findings from that time.

The vegetative state is a clinical condition of complete unawareness of the self and the environment, accompanied by sleep–wake cycles with either complete or partial preservation of hypothalamic and brain-stem autonomic functions. In addition, patients in a vegetative state show no evidence of sustained, reproducible, purposeful, or voluntary behavioural responses to visual, auditory, tactile or noxious stimuli; show no evidence of language comprehension or expression; have bowel and bladder incontinence; and have variably preserved cranial-nerve and spinal reflexes. We define persistent vegetative state as a vegetative state present one month after acute traumatic or nontraumatic brain injury or lasting for at least one month in patients with degenerative or metabolic disorders or developmental malformations.

...

Recovery of consciousness from a posttraumatic persistent vegetative state is unlikely after 12 months in adults and

UNAWARENESS | PROLONGED UNCONSCIOUSNESS

children. Recovery from a nontraumatic persistent vegetative state after three months is exceedingly rare in both adults and children. Patients with degenerative or metabolic disorders or congenital malformations who remain in a persistent vegetative state for several months are unlikely to recover consciousness.

More Dead than Dead
Kurt Gray, T Anne Knickman and Daniel M Wegner, 2011

> American psychologists Kurt Gray, T Anne Knickman and Daniel M Wegner conducted two experiments to identify how people perceive the mental capacity of a fictional patient in different scenarios (the patient either recovers, dies or enters a persistent vegetative state (PVS)). In a third experiment, participants considered the likely impact if they themselves were to die, or enter a PVS.

In these experiments, people consistently viewed the persistent vegetative state (PVS) as something less than dead: they ascribed less mind to people in a PVS (Experiments 1–3) and saw it as worse than death (Experiment 3). Apparent reasons for such perceptions are afterlife beliefs and the tendency to focus on the bodies of PVS patients (Experiment 2).

Although there may also be other variables operating in perceptions of PVS patients, such as liking and familiarity[1], these results are consistent with a number of previous studies that highlight the power of afterlife beliefs[2] and conceiving people as either minds or bodies[3]. Indeed, many health-care professions advocate such a separation between mind and body[4], suggesting that even doctors may see PVS patients as having less mind than the dead. Some research, however, suggests that doctors may ascribe additional mind to those in vegetative states[5], perhaps because frequent contact with such patients allows opportunity to ascribe mind[6]. Nevertheless, there is reason to believe that most people will at least implicitly have trouble ascribing mind to PVS patients.

Most importantly, these results suggest that people's perceptions of PVS are out of step with objective biological functioning. A person in PVS, after all, is more functional than a dead person. Yet people seem to have difficulty thinking about such intermediate states in which modern medical technology blurs the line between life and death, allowing people to remain in limbo. As this limbo defies easy categorisation, people rely more on intuition than on neurological evidence, which can lead to ethical quandaries[7]. People ascribe moral rights on the basis of mind, and if PVS patients are perceived to have less mind than the dead, then they may also be granted fewer rights than the dead[8]. Moreover, if people would rather be dead than in PVS, then it suggests that caregivers should be more willing to remove life support. Of course, there are other factors involved in end of life decisions[9], but these data do highlight one irony: people high in religiosity are more likely to see PVS as worse off than death, but are also more likely to advocate keeping such patients alive on life support. This echoes previous findings that religious attitudes and behaviours can be discrepant when the end of life is concerned: those high in religiosity will most aggressively pursue end of life care despite the belief that souls live on[10].

Rather than resolve the ethical debates posed by Terri Schiavo and other PVS patients, these experiments suggest another layer of complexity – lay intuitions driven by dualism distort conceptions of vegetative states. In terms of influencing policy, these findings suggest debates over the fate of such patients may hinge upon our tendency to see minds and bodies as distinct and competing conceptions of others. Advocates of terminating life support may frame vegetative patients as bodies, while those who advocate continued life support may highlight their mental capacities. Either way, these results suggest that for vegetative patients, life or death may depend more upon the mind of the person making the decision than the mind of the patient.

1 Epley N et al. On seeing human: a three-factor theory of anthropomorphism. Psychol Rev 2007;114(4):864–86; Kozak MN et al. What do I think you're doing? Action identification and mind attribution. J Pers Soc Psychol 2006;90(4):543–55.
2 Bering JM, Bjorklund DF. The natural emergence of reasoning about the afterlife as a developmental regularity. Dev Psychol 2004;40(2):217–33.
3 Demertzi A et al. Dualism persists in the science of mind. Ann N Y Acad Sci 2009;1157:1–9; Fahrenberg J, Cheetham M. The mind-body problem as seen by students of different disciplines. Journal Conscious Stud 2000;7(5):47–59.
4 Demertzi A et al. Dualism persists in the science of mind. Ann N Y Acad Sci 2009;1157:1–9.
5 Demertzi A et al. Different beliefs about pain perception in the vegetative and minimally conscious states: a European survey of medical and paramedical professionals. Prog Brain Res 2009;177:329–38.
6 Epley N, Waytz A. Mind perception. In ST Fiske et al. (eds). The Handbook of Social Psychology. 5th edn. New York: Wiley; 2009.
7 Luce JM. Physicians do not have a responsibility to provide futile or unreasonable care if a patient or family insists. Crit Care Med 1995;23(4):760–6; Stanley JM. The Appleton consensus: suggested international guidelines for decisions to forego medical treatment. J Med Ethics 1989;15(3):129–36.
8 Gonzalez JA. Modern medicine, murder, and the mind. J Leg Med 2009;30(4):529–43.
9 Van der Heide A et al. End-of-life decision-making in six European countries: descriptive study. Lancet 2003;362(9381):345–50.
10 Phelps AC et al. Association between religious coping and use of intensive life-prolonging care near death among patients with advanced cancer. JAMA 2009;301(11):1140–7.

'Locked Inside a Box'
Roger Highfield, 2014

> British neuroscientist Adrian Owen and Belgian neurolo-
> gist Steven Laureys have used brain-scanning technology
> to communicate with patients clinically considered to
> be unaware of themselves and their environment. These
> extracts from an article describing their work explore
> opinions about these developments and their life-changing
> consequences.

"Imagine you wake up, locked inside a box," says Adrian
Owen. "It's only just big enough to hold your body but sufficiently small that you can't move.

"It's a perfect fit, down to every last one of your fingers and
toes. It's a strange box because you can listen to absolutely
everything going on around you, yet your voice cannot be
heard. In fact, the box fits so tightly around your face and
lips that you can't speak, or make a noise. Although you can
see everything going on around the box, the world outside is
oblivious to what's going on inside.

"Inside, there's plenty of time to think. At first, this feels
like a game, even one that is strangely amusing. Then, reality
sets in. You're trapped. You see and hear your family lamenting
your fate. Over the years, the carers forget to turn on the TV.
You're too cold. Then you're too hot. You're always thirsty. The
visits of your friends and family dwindle. Your partner moves
on. And there's nothing you can do about it."

...

Owen and Laureys were trying to find a reliable way to communicate with patients in a vegetative state, including Gillian*. In
July 2005, this 23-year-old had been crossing a road, chatting
on her mobile phone. She was struck by two cars. Yet, though
she had been diagnosed as vegetative, there was something

UNAWARENESS | MINIMAL CONSCIOUSNESS

about her that caught the attention of Martin Coleman of the University of Cambridge Impaired Consciousness Research Group, who submitted her for study by Owen.

Five months later, a strange stroke of serendipity allowed Gillian to unlock her box. The key arose from a systematic study Owen started with Laureys in 2005. They had asked healthy volunteers to imagine doing different things, such as singing songs or conjuring up the face of their mother. Then Owen had another idea. "I just had a hunch," he says. "I asked a healthy control to imagine playing tennis. Then I asked her to imagine walking through the rooms of her house." Imagining tennis activates part of the cortex, called the supplementary motor area, involved in the mental simulation of movements. But imagining walking around the house activates the parahippocampal gyrus in the core of the brain, the posterior parietal lobe, and the lateral premotor cortex. The two patterns of activity were as distinct as a 'yes' and a 'no'. So, if people were asked to imagine tennis for 'yes' and walking around the house for 'no', they could answer questions via fMRI.

Gazing into Gillian's 'vegetative' brain with the brain scanner, he asked her to imagine the same things – and saw strikingly similar activation patterns to the healthy volunteers. It was an electric moment. Owen could read her mind.

Gillian's case, published in the journal *Science* in 2006, made front-page headlines around the world. The result provoked wonder and, of course, disbelief. "Broadly speaking, I received two types of email from my peers," says Owen. "They either said 'This is amazing – well done!' or 'How could you possibly say this woman is conscious?'"

As the old saw goes, extraordinary claims require extraordinary evidence. The sceptics countered that it was wrong to make these 'radical inferences' when there could be a more straightforward interpretation. Daniel Greenberg, a psychologist at the University of California, Los Angeles, suggested that "the brain activity was unconsciously triggered by the last word of the instructions, which always referred to the item to be imagined".

Parashkev Nachev, a neurologist now at University College London, says he objected to Owen's 2006 paper not on grounds of implausibility or a flawed statistical analysis but because of "errors of inference". Although a conscious brain, when imagining tennis, triggers a certain pattern of activation, it does not necessarily mean that the same pattern of activation signifies consciousness. The same brain area can be activated in many circumstances, Nachev says, with or without any conscious correlate. Moreover, he argues that Gillian was not really offered a true choice to think about playing tennis. Just as a lack of response could be because of an inability to respond or a decision not to cooperate, a direct response to a simple instruction could be a conscious decision or a reflex. Nachev says that he is weary of stating, as he has time and again to the media, that profound conceptual issues with the techniques used to redefine this penumbra of consciousness remain unresolved.

What is needed is less philosophising and more data, says Owen. A follow-up study published in 2010 by Owen, Laureys and colleagues tested 54 patients with a clinical diagnosis of being in a vegetative state or a minimally conscious state; five responded in the same way as Gillian. Four of them were supposedly in a vegetative state at admission. Owen, Schiff and Laureys have explored alternative explanations of what they observed and, for example, acknowledge that the brain areas they study when they interrogate patients can be activated in other ways. But the 2010 paper ruled out such automatic behaviours as an explanation, they say: the activations persist too long to signify anything other than intent. Owen is grateful to his critics. They spurred him on, for instance to develop a method for asking patients questions that only they would know how to answer. "You cannot communicate unconsciously – it is just not possible," he says. "We have won that argument."

Since Owen's 2006 *Science* paper, studies in Belgium, the UK, the USA and Canada suggest that a significant proportion of patients who were classified as vegetative in recent years have been misdiagnosed – Owen estimates perhaps as many as 20 per cent. Schiff, who weighs up the extent of misdiagnosis a different way, goes further. Based on recent studies, he says around 40 per cent of patients thought to be vegetative are, when examined more closely, partly aware. Among this group of supposedly vegetative patients are those who are revealed by scanners to be able to communicate and should be diagnosed as locked-in, if they are fully conscious, or minimally conscious, if their abilities wax and wane. But Schiff believes the remainder will have to be defined another way altogether, since being aware does not necessarily mean being able to use mental imagery. Nor does being aware enough to follow a command mean possessing the ability to communicate.

In 2009, Laureys's team asked one of the original group of 54 patients that he and Owen had studied – patient 23 – a series of yes-or-no questions. It was the usual drill: imagine playing tennis for yes, navigating the house for no. The Liège patient, who had been in a vegetative state for five years, was able to answer five of six questions about his earlier life – and all of those were correct. Had he been on holiday to a certain place prior to his injury? Was such-and-such his father's name? It was an exciting moment, said Laureys. "We were stunned," adds Owen, who helped independently score the tests. "By showing us that he was conscious and aware, patient 23 moved himself from the 'do not resuscitate' category to the 'not allowed to die' category. Did we save his life? No. He saved his own life."

*Some names have been changed to protect identities

'Awareness under Anaesthesia'
The Royal College of Anaesthetists and the Association of Anaesthetists of Great Britain and Ireland, 2014

> The Royal College of Anaesthetists' fifth National Audit Project, edited by J J Pandit and T M Cook, focused on a common fear: accidental awareness during general anaesthesia. The report estimates that 1 in every 20,000 anaesthetised patients reports awareness, with an increased likelihood for cardiothoracic and Caesarean surgeries.

At the age of twelve, I thought I was about to die.

I was wheeled into a fairly routine orthodontic operation, not expecting anything untoward to happen. I was quite a grown up twelve-year-old, the size of a small adult, but I was aware the medical professionals were treating me like a much younger child, so played along with them, for the sake of an easy life. I counted down from ten, as you do, and presumably fell asleep.

Suddenly, I was aware something had gone very wrong. I could hear what was going on around me, and I realised with horror that I had woken up in the middle of the operation, but couldn't move a muscle. I heard the banal chatter of the surgeons, and I was aware of many people in the room bustling about, doing their everyday clinical jobs and minding their own business, with absolutely no idea of the cataclysmic event that was unfolding from my point of view. While they fiddled, I lay there, frantically trying to decide whether I was about to die, and what options were open to me.

I rapidly audited each part of my body, to see if anything worked at all. I had seen films about this sort of thing, I thought to myself. People are paralysed for their whole lives and sobbing relatives congregate by the bedside for years at a time until the damaged person finally manages to blink. Good! I said to myself. Let's try the eyes first. No result. Let's try the toes, I thought. No result. Oh dear, I thought. This is a very serious situation. Systematically I went through each body part again, muscle by muscle, nerve by nerve, sinew by sinew, willing something, anything to react. At first, it felt as though nothing would ever work again, as though the anaesthetist had removed everything from me apart from my soul. On the next full body audit, suddenly my arm was free, with a mind of its own, and I successfully punched the surgeon in the face to get his attention. "Oh dear!" he said, in a rather flat, uninterested voice, "We have a fighter." Then the pace of work sped up and finally I was taken to recovery. Once I had gathered my wits a little, and worked out how to speak with a huge plate in my mouth; I said, "I woke up in there! I woke up during the operation!"

This would be something I would continue to say for the rest of my time in hospital, and each time I said it, I was told this couldn't be true, that it was my imagination, that I was mistaken. When I related surgically-related conversations to the theatre team, they went a little white, but continued to deny what had happened. They denied it to my mother, and in doing so, left me alone to deal with the decades-long fallout of my putative near death experience.

There was no internet or Childline then, so when something dramatic and terrifying happened, children were more or less on their own. Slowly, over the years, I tried to make sense of events. Each time I needed an operation subsequently, I would tell the anaesthetists of the chain of events, and they would reveal a little more of what might have gone wrong, and promise profusely that I would be safe in their hands. This helped on an intellectual level, and for that I am very grateful. However, they could not help with the recurrent nightmare, where a 'Dr Who' style monster leapt on me and paralysed me. That went on for fifteen years or so, until I suddenly made the connection with feeling paralysed during the operation. After that I was freed of the nightmare and finally liberated from the more stressful aspects of the event.

The Effects of Chloroform
Richard Tennant Cooper, c.1912

British artist Richard Tennant Cooper (1885–1957) gives this patient under anaesthesia a rather vulnerable air, complete with crouching surgical demons not dissimilar from earlier incubus and nightmare imagery.

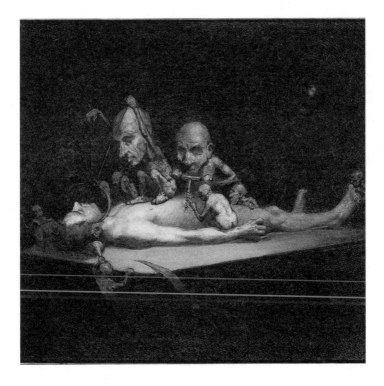

The Halving
Robin Robertson, 2012

Scottish poet Robin Robertson (b. 1955) penned these
verses after undergoing an operation to replace one of the
valves in his heart. A bypass machine kept him alive while
his heart was stopped.

(Royal Brompton Hospital, 1986)

General anaesthesia; a median sternotomy
achieved by sternal saw; the ribs
held aghast by retractor; the tubes
and cannulae drawing the blood
to the reservoir, and its bubbler;
the struggling aorta
cross-clamped, the heart
chilled and stopped and left to dry.
The incompetent bicuspid valve excised,
the new one – a carbon-coated disc, housed
expensively in a cage of tantalum –
is broken from its sterile pouch
then heavily implanted into the native heart,
bolstered, seated with sutures.
The aorta freed, the heart re-started.
The blood allowed back
after its time abroad
circulating in the machine.
The rib-spreader relaxed
and the plumbing removed, the breast-bone
lashed with sternal wires, the incision closed.

Four hours I'd been away: out of my body.
Made to die then jerked back to the world.
The distractions of delirium
came and went and then,
as the morphine drained, I was left with a split
chest that ground and grated on itself.
Over the pain, a blackness rose and swelled;
'pump-head' is what some call it
 – debris from the bypass machine
migrating to the brain – but it felt
more interesting than that.
Halved and unhelmed,
I have been away, I said to the ceiling,
and now I am not myself.

'Separated from His Senses'
Henry David Thoreau, 1851

Writing in his journal after taking ether for a dental procedure, American author Henry David Thoreau (1817–1862) described the then novel experience of anaesthesia.

By taking the ether the other day I was convinced how far asunder a man could be separated from his senses. You are told that it will make you unconscious, but no one can imagine what it is to be unconscious – how far removed from the state of consciousness and all that we call 'this world' – until he has experienced it. The value of the experiment is that it does give you experience of an interval as between one life and another, – a greater space than you ever travelled. You are a sane mind without organs, – groping for organs, – which if it did not soon recover its old senses would get new ones. You expand like a seed in the ground. You exist in your roots, like a tree in the winter. If you have an inclination to travel, take the ether; you go beyond the furthest star.

It is not necessary for them to take ether, who in their sane and waking hours are ever translated by a thought; nor for them to see with their hindheads, who sometimes see from their foreheads; nor listen to the spiritual knockings, who attend to the intimations of reason and conscience.

The Effects of Liquid Chloroform
Unknown artist, 1840s

The popular story of the discovery of chloroform's anaesthetic properties describes Scottish obstetrician James Young Simpson (1811–1870) inhaling the drug at a dinner party. Simpson's maid is said to have discovered the physician and his fellow diners asleep.

'A Numbness of Spirit'
Guy de Maupassant, 1888

French writer Guy de Maupassant's (1850–1893) *Afloat*
purports to be a diary of the author's nine-day cruise around
the French Riviera. In this excerpt Maupassant inhales ether
to dull the pain of a dreadful headache.

A sick headache, the dreadful pain that racks in a way no
torture could equal, shatters the head, drives one crazy, bewil-
ders the ideas, and scatters the memory like dust before the
wind; a sick headache had laid hold of me, and I was perforce
obliged to lie down in my bunk with a bottle of ether under
my nostrils.

After a few minutes, I fancied I heard a vague murmur
which soon became a kind of buzzing, and it seemed as if all
the interior of my body became light, as light as air, as though
it were melting into vapour.

Then followed a numbness of spirit, a drowsy, comfortable
state, in spite of the persisting pain, which, however, ceased to
be acute. It was now a pain which one could consent to bear,
and not any longer the terrible tearing agony, against which the
whole tortured body rises in protest.

Soon the strange, and delightful sensation of vacuum I had
in my chest extended, and reached my limbs, which in their
turn became light, light as though flesh and bone had melted
away and skin only remained; just enough skin to permit of
my feeling the sweetness of life, and enjoy my repose. Now I
found that I no longer suffered. Pain had disappeared, melted,
vanished into air. And I hear voices, four voices, two dialogues,
without understanding the words. At times they were but
indistinct sounds, at other times a word or two reached me.
But I soon recognised that these were but the accentuated
buzzing of my own ears. I was not sleeping, I was awake, I

ANAESTHESIA

understood, I felt, I reasoned with a clearness, a penetration and power which were quite extraordinary; and a joyousness of spirit, a strange intoxication, produced by the tenfold increase of my mental faculties.

It was not a dream like that created by haschich, nor the sickly visions produced by opium; it was a prodigious keenness of reasoning, a new manner of seeing, of judging, of estimating things and life, with the absolute consciousness, the certitude that this manner was the true one.

And the old simile of the Scriptures, suddenly came back to my mind. It seemed to me that I had tasted of the tree of life, that all mystery was unveiled, so strongly did I feel the power of this new, strange, and irrefutable logic. And numberless arguments, reasonings, proofs, rose up in my mind, to be, however, immediately upset by some proof, some reasoning, some argument yet more powerful. My brain had become a battle-field of ideas. I was a superior being, armed with an invincible intelligence, and I enjoyed prodigious happiness in the sensation of my power.

This state lasted a long, long time. I still inhaled the fumes of my ether bottle. Suddenly, I perceived that it was empty. And I again began to suffer.

'A Stupefying and Overpowering Smell of Chloroform'
Arthur Conan Doyle, 1911

> Like many writers, Arthur Conan Doyle (1859–1930) spotted the dramatic potential of a drug that could quickly render a character unconscious. He employed the literary device in several stories, including *The Disappearance of Lady Frances Carfax*. In this excerpt Sherlock Holmes and Dr Watson call on a Mr Peters, who recently took delivery of a coffin.

Our opponent opened the door.

"Fetch a policeman, Annie!" said he. There was a whisk of feminine skirts down the passage, and the hall door was opened and shut.

"Our time is limited, Watson," said Holmes. "If you try to stop us, Peters, you will most certainly get hurt. Where is that coffin which was brought into your house?"

"What do you want with the coffin? It is in use. There is a body in it."

"I must see the body."

"Never with my consent."

"Then without it." With a quick movement Holmes pushed the fellow to one side and passed into the hall. A door half open stood immediately before us. We entered. It was the dining-room. On the table, under a half-lit chandelier, the coffin was lying. Holmes turned up the gas and raised the lid. Deep down in the recesses of the coffin lay an emaciated figure. The glare from the lights above beat down upon an aged and withered face. By no possible process of cruelty, starvation, or disease could this worn-out wreck be the still beautiful Lady Frances. Holmes's face showed his amazement, and also his relief.

"Thank God!" he muttered. "It's someone else."

"Ah, you've blundered badly for once, Mr Sherlock Holmes," said Peters, who had followed us into the room.

"Who is the dead woman?"

"Well, if you really must know, she is an old nurse of my wife's, Rose Spender her name, whom we found in the Brixton Workhouse Infirmary. We brought her round here, called in Dr Horsom, of 13 Firbank Villas – mind you take the address, Mr Holmes – and had her carefully tended, as Christian folk should. On the third day she died – certificate says senile decay – but that's only the doctor's opinion, and, of course, you know better. We ordered her funeral to be carried out by Stimson and Co., of the Kennington Road, who will bury her at eight o'clock to-morrow morning. Can you pick any hole in that, Mr Holmes? You've made a silly blunder, and you may as well own up to it. I'd give something for a photograph of your gaping, staring face when you pulled aside that lid expecting to see the Lady Frances Carfax and only found a poor old woman of ninety."

Holmes's expression was as impassive as ever under the jeers of his antagonist, but his clenched hands betrayed his acute annoyance.

"I am going through your house," said he.

"Are you, though!" cried Peters as a woman's voice and heavy steps sounded in the passage. "We'll soon see about that. This way, officers, if you please. These men have forced their way into my house, and I cannot get rid of them. Help me to put them out."

A sergeant and a constable stood in the doorway. Holmes drew his card from his case.

"This is my name and address. This is my friend, Dr Watson."

"Bless you, sir, we know you very well," said the sergeant, "but you can't stay here without a warrant."

"Of course not. I quite understand that."

"Arrest him!" cried Peters.

"We know where to lay our hands on this gentleman if he is wanted," said the sergeant, majestically, "but you'll have to go, Mr Holmes."

"Yes, Watson, we shall have to go."

A minute later we were in the street once more. Holmes was as cool as ever, but I was hot with anger and humiliation. The sergeant had followed us.

"Sorry, Mr Holmes, but that's the law."

"Exactly, Sergeant; you could not do otherwise."

"I expect there was good reason for your presence there. If there is anything I can do – "

"It's a missing lady, sergeant, and we think she is in that house. I expect a warrant presently."

"Then I'll keep my eye on the parties, Mr Holmes. If anything comes along, I will surely let you know."

It was only nine o'clock, and we were off full cry upon the trail at once. First we drove to Brixton Workhouse Infirmary, where we found that it was indeed the truth that a charitable couple had called some days before, that they had claimed an imbecile old woman as a former servant, and that they had obtained permission to take her away with them. No surprise was expressed at the news that she had since died.

The doctor was our next goal. He had been called in, had found the woman dying of pure senility, had actually seen her pass away, and had signed the certificate in due form. "I assure you that everything was perfectly normal and there was no room for foul play in the matter," said he. Nothing in the house had struck him as suspicious, save that for people of their class it was remarkable that they should have no servant. So far and no further went the doctor.

Finally, we found our way to Scotland Yard. There had been difficulties of procedure in regard to the warrant. Some delay was inevitable. The magistrate's signature might not be obtained until next morning. If Holmes would call about nine he could go down with Lestrade and see it acted upon. So ended the day, save that near midnight our friend, the sergeant, called to say that he had seen flickering lights here and there in the windows of the great dark house, but that no one had left it and none had entered. We could but pray for patience, and wait for the morrow.

Sherlock Holmes was too irritable for conversation and too restless for sleep. I left him smoking hard, with his heavy, dark brows knotted together, and his long, nervous fingers tapping upon the arms of his chair, as he turned over in his mind every possible solution of the mystery. Several times in the course of the night I heard him prowling about the house. Finally, just after I had been called in the morning, he rushed into my room. He was in his dressing-gown, but his pale, hollow-eyed face told me that his night had been a sleepless one.

"What time was the funeral? Eight, was it not?" he asked, eagerly. "Well, it is seven-twenty now. Good heavens, Watson, what has become of any brains that God has given me? Quick, man, quick! It's life or death – a hundred chances on death to one on life. I'll never forgive myself, never, if we are too late!"

Five minutes had not passed before we were flying in a hansom down Baker Street. But even so it was twenty-five to eight as we passed Big Ben, and eight struck as we tore down the Brixton Road. But others were late as well as we. Ten minutes after the hour the hearse was still standing at the door of the house, and even as our foaming horse came to a halt the coffin, supported by three men, appeared on the threshold. Holmes darted forward and barred their way.

"Take it back!" he cried, laying his hand on the breast of the foremost. "Take it back this instant!"

"What the devil do you mean? Once again I ask you, where is your warrant?" shouted the furious Peters, his big red face glaring over the farther end of the coffin.

"The warrant is on its way. The coffin shall remain in the house until it comes."

The authority in Holmes's voice had its effect upon the bearers. Peters had suddenly vanished into the house, and they obeyed these new orders. "Quick, Watson, quick! Here is a screw-driver!" he shouted, as the coffin was replaced upon the table. "Here's one for you, my man! A sovereign if the lid comes off in a minute! Ask no questions – work away! That's good! Another! And another! Now pull all together! It's giving! It's giving! Ah, that does it at last!"

With a united effort we tore off the coffin-lid. As we did so there came from the inside a stupefying and overpowering smell of chloroform. A body lay within, its head all wreathed in cotton-wool, which had been soaked in the narcotic. Holmes plucked it off and disclosed the statuesque face of a handsome and spiritual woman of middle age. In an instant he had passed his arm round the figure and raised her to a sitting position.

"Is she gone, Watson? Is there a spark left? Surely we are not too late!"

For half an hour it seemed that we were. What with actual suffocation, and what with the poisonous fumes of the chloroform, the Lady Frances seemed to have passed the last point of recall. And then, at last, with artificial respiration, with injected ether, with every device that science could suggest, some flutter of life, some quiver of the eyelids, some dimming of a mirror, spoke of the slowly returning life. A cab had driven up, and Holmes, parting the blind, looked out at it. "Here is Lestrade with his warrant," said he. "He will find that his birds have flown. And here," he added as a heavy step hurried along the passage, "is someone who has a better right to nurse this lady than we have. Good morning, Mr Green; I think that the sooner we can move the Lady Frances the better. Meanwhile, the funeral may proceed, and the poor old woman who still lies in that coffin may go to her last resting-place alone."

L'Inhumation Précipitée
Antoine Joseph Wiertz, 1854

When Belgian artist Antoine Wiertz (1806–1865) visited cholera-stricken Naples in 1837, sick – but not yet dead – people were being hastily buried in order to control the disease. Cholera's death-like symptoms commonly led to mistaken confirmations of death, generating a widespread fear of premature burial.

PREMATURE BURIAL | CONFIRMATION OF DEATH

'Sheer Terror'
Edgar Allan Poe, 1844

American author Edgar Allan Poe (1809–1849) included several accounts of those entombed alive in his short story *The Premature Burial*. This extract also considers the boundaries between life and death.

To be buried while alive is, beyond question, the most terrific of these extremes which has ever fallen to the lot of mere mortality. That it has frequently, very frequently, so fallen will scarcely be denied by those who think. The boundaries which divide Life from Death are at best shadowy and vague. Who shall say where the one ends, and where the other begins? We know that there are diseases in which occur total cessations of all the apparent functions of vitality, and yet in which these cessations are merely suspensions, properly so called. They are only temporary pauses in the incomprehensible mechanism. A certain period elapses, and some unseen mysterious principle again sets in motion the magic pinions and the wizard wheels. The silver cord was not for ever loosed, nor the golden bowl irreparably broken. But where, meantime, was the soul?

Apart, however, from the inevitable conclusion, *a priori* that such causes must produce such effects, – that the well-known occurrence of such cases of suspended animation must naturally give rise, now and then, to premature interments, – apart from this consideration, we have the direct testimony of medical and ordinary experience to prove that a vast number of such interments have actually taken place. I might refer at once, if necessary, to a hundred well-authenticated instances. One of very remarkable character, and of which the circumstances may be fresh in the memory of some of my readers, occurred, not very long ago, in the neighbouring city of Baltimore, where it occasioned a painful, intense, and widely-extended excitement.

The wife of one of the most respectable citizens – a lawyer of eminence and a member of Congress – was seized with a sudden and unaccountable illness, which completely baffled the skill of her physicians. After much suffering she died, or was supposed to die. No one suspected, indeed, or had reason to suspect, that she was not actually dead. She presented all the ordinary appearances of death. The face assumed the usual pinched and sunken outline. The lips were of the usual marble pallor. The eyes were lustreless. There was no warmth. Pulsation had ceased. For three days the body was preserved unburied, during which it had acquired a stony rigidity. The funeral, in short, was hastened, on account of the rapid advance of what was supposed to be decomposition.

The lady was deposited in her family vault, which, for three subsequent years, was undisturbed. At the expiration of this term it was opened for the reception of a sarcophagus; – but, alas! how fearful a shock awaited the husband, who, personally, threw open the door! As its portals swung outwardly back, some white-apparelled object fell rattling within his arms. It was the skeleton of his wife in her yet unmoulded shroud.

A careful investigation rendered it evident that she had revived within two days after her entombment; that her struggles within the coffin had caused it to fall from a ledge, or shelf to the floor, where it was so broken as to permit her escape. A lamp which had been accidentally left, full of oil, within the tomb, was found empty; it might have been exhausted, however, by evaporation. On the uppermost of the steps which led down into the dread chamber was a large fragment of the coffin, with which it seemed that she had endeavoured to arrest attention by striking the iron door. While thus occupied, she probably swooned, or possibly died, through sheer terror; and, in falling, her shroud became entangled in some iron-work which projected interiorly. Thus she remained, and thus she rotted, erect.

Count Karnice-Karnicki's Invention
Unknown artist, 1905

Russian nobleman Count Michel de Karnice-Karnicki
patented a security coffin in 1897, selling the device for 12
shillings. If the corpse's chest or arms moved, a bell rung,
a flag waved and a tube opened to allow air into the coffin.
The casket's initial appeal was soon extinguished after the
test burial of a live assistant failed to set off the alarms.

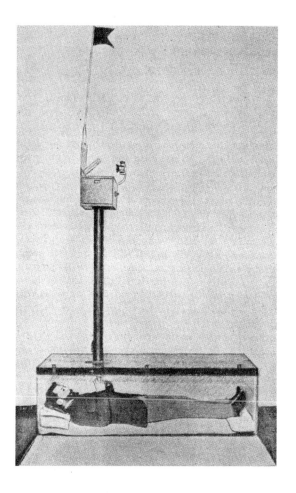

'Then There Was Silence'
Edward Henry Bickersteth, 1866

Church of England minister Edward Henry Bickersteth's
(1825–1906) epic poem *Yesterday, To-day, and For Ever* is said
to have sold 80,000 copies. This extract, entitled 'The seer's
death, and descent to Hades', describes the narrator's final
moments of life.

Then there was silence: and my children knelt
Around my bed – our latest family prayer.
Listen – it is eleven striking. Then
I whisper'd to my wife, "The time is short;
I hear the Spirit and the Bride say, Come,
And Jesus answering, 'I come quickly.' Listen."
And as she wiped the death-dews from my brow,
She falter'd, "He is very near," and I
Could only faintly say, "Amen, amen."
And then my power of utterance was gone:
I beckon'd and was speechless: I was more
Than ankle deep in Jordan's icy stream.
My children stood upon its utmost verge,
Gazing imploringly, persuasively,
While the words, "Dear, dear father," now and then
Would drop, like dew, from their unconscious lips.
My gentle wife, with love stronger than death,
Was leaning over those cold gliding waves.
I heard them speaking, but could make no sign;
I saw them weeping, but could shed no tear;
I felt their touch upon my flickering pulse,
Their breath upon my cheek, but I could give
No answering pressure to the fond hands press'd

In mine. So rapidly the river-bed
Shelved downward, I had pass'd or almost pass'd
Beyond the interchange of loving signs
Into the very world of love itself.

'As One Already Dead'
Ambrose Bierce, 1890

At the conclusion of American journalist Ambrose Bierce's
(1842–1914) short story *An Occurrence at Owl Creek Bridge*
Peyton Farquhar stands on the edge of a railroad bridge,
ready to be executed by hanging. His thoughts indicate he
may be in a state of heightened consciousness.

As Peyton Farquhar fell straight downward through the bridge,
he lost consciousness and was as one already dead. From this
state he was awakened – ages later, it seemed to him – by the
pain of a sharp pressure upon his throat, followed by a sense
of suffocation. Keen, poignant agonies seemed to shoot from
his neck downward through every fibre of his body and limbs.
These pains appeared to flash along well defined lines of
ramification and to beat with an inconceivably rapid period-
icity. They seemed like streams of pulsating fire heating him to
an intolerable temperature. As to his head, he was conscious
of nothing but a feeling of fullness – of congestion. These
sensations were unaccompanied by thought. The intellectual
part of his nature was already effaced; he had power only to
feel, and feeling was torment. He was conscious of motion.
Encompassed in a luminous cloud, of which he was now
merely the fiery heart, without material substance, he swung
through unthinkable arcs of oscillation, like a vast pendulum.
Then all at once, with terrible suddenness, the light about him
shot upward with the noise of a loud plash; a frightful roaring

DYING | HEIGHTENED CONSCIOUSNESS

was in his ears, and all was cold and dark. The power of
thought was restored; he knew that the rope had broken and he
had fallen into the stream. There was no additional strangula-
tion; the noose about his neck was already suffocating him and
kept the water from his lungs. To die of hanging at the bottom
of a river! – the idea seemed to him ludicrous. He opened his
eyes in the blackness and saw above him a gleam of light, but
how distant, how inaccessible! He was still sinking, for the
light became fainter and fainter until it was a mere glimmer.
Then it began to grow and brighten, and he knew that he was
rising toward the surface – knew it with reluctance, for he
was now very comfortable. "To be hanged and drowned," he
thought, "that is not so bad; but I do not wish to be shot. No;
I will not be shot; that is not fair."

He was not conscious of an effort, but a sharp pain in
his wrist apprised him that he was trying to free his hands.
He gave the struggle his attention, as an idler might observe
the feat of a juggler, without interest in the outcome. What
splendid effort! – what magnificent, what superhuman
strength! Ah, that was a fine endeavour! Bravo! The cord fell
away; his arms parted and floated upward, the hands dimly
seen on each side in the growing light. He watched them with
a new interest as first one and then the other pounced upon
the noose at his neck. They tore it away and thrust it fiercely
aside, its undulations resembling those of a water snake. "Put
it back, put it back!" He thought he shouted these words to his
hands, for the undoing of the noose had been succeeded by
the direst pang that he had yet experienced. His neck ached
horribly; his brain was on fire, his heart, which had been
fluttering faintly, gave a great leap, trying to force itself out at
his mouth. His whole body was racked and wrenched with
an insupportable anguish! But his disobedient hands gave no
heed to the command. They beat the water vigorously with
quick, downward strokes, forcing him to the surface.

He felt his head emerge; his eyes were blinded by the sunlight; his chest expanded convulsively, and with a supreme and crowning agony his lungs engulfed a great draught of air, which instantly he expelled in a shriek!

He was now in full possession of his physical senses. They were, indeed, preternaturally keen and alert. Something in the awful disturbance of his organic system had so exalted and refined them that they made record of things never before perceived. He felt the ripples upon his face and heard their separate sounds as they struck. He looked at the forest on the bank of the stream, saw the individual trees, the leaves and the veining of each leaf – he saw the very insects upon them, the locusts, the brilliant-bodied flies, the grey spiders stretching their webs from twig to twig. He noted the prismatic colours in all the dewdrops upon a million blades of grass. The humming of the gnats that danced above the eddies of the stream, the beating of the dragon flies' wings, the strokes of the water spiders' legs, like oars which had lifted their boat – all these made audible music. A fish slid along beneath his eyes and he heard the rush of its body parting the water.

He had come to the surface facing down the stream; in a moment the visible world seemed to wheel slowly round, himself the pivotal point, and he saw the bridge, the fort, the soldiers upon the bridge, the captain, the sergeant, the two privates, his executioners. They were in silhouette against the blue sky. They shouted and gesticulated, pointing at him; the captain had drawn his pistol, but did not fire; the others were unarmed. Their movements were grotesque and horrible, their forms gigantic.

Suddenly he heard a sharp report and something struck the water smartly within a few inches of his head, spattering his face with spray. He heard a second report, and saw one of the sentinels with his rifle at his shoulder, a light cloud of blue smoke rising from the muzzle. The man in the water saw the eye of the man on the bridge gazing into his own through the sights of the rifle. He observed that it was a grey eye, and remembered having read that grey eyes were keenest, and that all famous marksmen had them. Nevertheless, this one had missed.

A counter swirl had caught Farquhar and turned him half round; he was again looking at the forest on the bank opposite the fort. The sound of a clear, high voice in a monotonous singsong now rang out behind him and came across the water with a distinctness that pierced and subdued all other sounds, even the beating of the ripples in his ears. Although no soldier, he had frequented camps enough to know the dread significance of that deliberate, drawling, aspirated chant; the lieutenant on shore was taking a part in the morning's work. How coldly and pitilessly – with what an even, calm intonation, presaging, and enforcing tranquillity in the men – with what accurately measured intervals fell those cruel words:

"Attention, company... Shoulder arms... Ready... Aim... Fire."

Farquhar dived – dived as deeply as he could. The water roared in his ears like the voice of Niagara, yet he heard the dull thunder of the volley, and, rising again toward the surface, met shining bits of metal, singularly flattened, oscillating slowly downward. Some of them touched him on the face and hands, then fell away, continuing their descent. One lodged between his collar and neck; it was uncomfortably warm, and he snatched it out.

As he rose to the surface, gasping for breath, he saw that he had been a long time under water; he was perceptibly farther downstream – nearer to safety. The soldiers had almost finished reloading; the metal ramrods flashed all at once in the sunshine as they were drawn from the barrels, turned in the air, and thrust into their sockets. The two sentinels fired again, independently and ineffectually.

The hunted man saw all this over his shoulder; he was now swimming vigorously with the current. His brain was as energetic as his arms and legs; he thought with the rapidity of lightning.

"The officer," he reasoned, "will not make that martinet's error a second time. It is as easy to dodge a volley as a single shot. He has probably already given the command to fire at will. God help me, I cannot dodge them all!"

An appalling plash within two yards of him was followed by a loud, rushing sound, *diminuendo*, which seemed to travel back through the air to the fort and died in an explosion which stirred the very river to its deeps! A rising sheet of water, which curved over him, fell down upon him, blinded him, strangled him! The cannon had taken a hand in the game. As he shook his head free from the commotion of the smitten water he heard the deflected shot humming through the air ahead, and in an instant it was cracking and smashing the branches in the forest beyond.

"They will not do that again," he thought; "the next time they will use a charge of grape. I must keep my eye upon the gun; the smoke will apprise me – the report arrives too late; it lags behind the missile. That is a good gun."

Suddenly he felt himself whirled round and round – spinning like a top. The water, the banks, the forests, the now distant bridge, fort and men – all were commingled and blurred. Objects were represented by their colours only; circular horizontal streaks of colour – that was all he saw. He had been caught in a vortex and was being whirled on with a velocity of advance and gyration that made him giddy and sick. In a few moments he was flung upon the gravel at the foot of the left bank of the stream – the southern bank – and behind a projecting point which concealed him from his enemies. The sudden arrest of his motion, the abrasion of one of his hands on the gravel, restored him and he wept with delight. He dug his fingers into the sand, threw it over himself in handfuls and audibly blessed it. It looked like diamonds, rubies, emeralds; he could think of nothing beautiful which it did not resemble. The trees upon the bank were giant garden plants; he noted a definite order in their arrangement, inhaled the fragrance of their blooms. A strange, roseate light shone through the spaces among their trunks, and the wind made in their branches the music of aeolian harps. He had no wish to perfect his escape, was content to remain in that enchanting spot until retaken.

A whizz and a rattle of grapeshot among the branches high above his head roused him from his dream. The baffled cannoneer had fired him a random farewell. He sprang to his feet, rushed up the sloping bank, and plunged into the forest.

All that day he travelled, laying his course by the rounding sun. The forest seemed interminable; nowhere did he discover a break in it, not even a woodman's road. He had not known that he lived in so wild a region. There was something uncanny in the revelation.

By nightfall he was fatigued, footsore, famishing. The thought of his wife and children urged him on. At last he found a road which led him in what he knew to be the right direction. It was as wide and straight as a city street, yet it seemed untravelled. No fields bordered it, no dwelling anywhere. Not so much as the barking of a dog suggested human habitation. The black bodies of the great trees formed a straight wall on both sides, terminating on the horizon in a point, like a diagram in a lesson in perspective. Overhead, as he looked up through this rift in the wood, shone great golden stars looking unfamiliar and grouped in strange constellations. He was sure they were arranged in some order which had a secret and malign significance. The wood on either side was full of singular noises, among which – once, twice, and again – he distinctly heard whispers in an unknown tongue.

His neck was in pain and, lifting his hand to it, he found it horribly swollen. He knew that it had a circle of black where the rope had bruised it. His eyes felt congested; he could no longer close them. His tongue was swollen with thirst; he relieved its fever by thrusting it forward from between his teeth into the cool air. How softly the turf had carpeted the untravelled avenue! He could no longer feel the roadway beneath his feet!

Doubtless, despite his suffering, he fell asleep while walking, for now he sees another scene – perhaps he has merely recovered from a delirium. He stands at the gate of his own home. All is as he left it, and all bright and beautiful in the morning sunshine. He must have travelled the entire night. As he pushes open the gate and passes up the wide white walk, he sees a flutter of female garments; his wife, looking fresh and cool and sweet, steps down from the veranda to meet him. At the bottom of the steps she stands waiting, with a smile of ineffable joy, an attitude of matchless grace and dignity. Ah, how beautiful she is! He springs forward with extended arms. As he is about to clasp her, he feels a stunning blow upon the back of the neck; a blinding white light blazes all about him, with a sound like the shock of a cannon – then all is darkness and silence!

Peyton Farquhar was dead; his body, with a broken neck, swung gently from side to side beneath the timbers of the Owl Creek bridge.

Body and Mind Dissolving
Graham Coleman, 2008

Swiss psychiatrist Carl Jung described *The Tibetan Book of the Dead*, a collection of centuries-old writings in the Tibetan Buddhist tradition, as "a book of instructions for the dead and dying". Designed for use in the 49-day intermediate state between life and rebirth, these translated and edited verses from what is more accurately titled *The Great Liberation by Hearing in the Intermediate States* outline the physical and spiritual experiences at the moment of death.

During this process, each exhalation of breath
    will become increasingly protracted,
While all the blood of the body will converge in
    the 'life channel',
And then a single drop of blood will form at
    the heart centre.
In this way, the phenomenon called 'blackness'
    will occur,
Engulfing the suffocating mind in blackness,
And one will experience the sensation of falling
    into darkness, as if into an abyss.
At that point, 'attainment' will dissolve into the
    'subtle mind of near attainment',
And the seven patterns of conceptual thought
    that originate from delusion will cease.

During this process, the mouth will open, and
    the eyes will roll upwards,
Exposing their pale underside.
External appearances will fade, as during the
    setting of the sun,

And finally the sense faculties, memory,
and perceptions will all cease,
Whereupon, all external appearances will be
absorbed into blackness.
At that point, the exhaled breath will extend
from the body by a cubit,
And all internal appearances will also come
to resemble darkness.

Then, the blood in the heart will form two drops,
The head will stoop,
And the exhaled breath will extend from the
body by an arrow-length.
Following this, the blood in the centre of the
heart will form three drops,
And, with HIKA-like gasps, the exhaled breath
will extend from the body by a double arm-span.
Then, the external breath will cease, and, engulfed
by blackness, one will become unconscious.
Then, the white and red 'generative essences'
will meet together at the heart,
And, as this occurs, one will swoon into a state
of blissfulness.
Thus, consciousness dissolves into inner radiance,
Engendering the experience of the 'coemergent delight'.
At this point, awareness dissolves into actual reality,
at the centre of the heart, like the meeting of
mother and child.
It is at this time that the inner breath will also cease,
And the vital energy and mind will rest in the
central channel.

Raising Lazarus from the Tomb
Unknown artist, 1510

The story of Jesus bringing Lazarus back to life after the corpse had lain four days in a tomb was first told in the Gospel of St John. It is almost certainly the Christian miracle most portrayed in art, having been a subject for such diverse interpreters as Giotto, Rembrandt, William Blake and Vincent van Gogh.

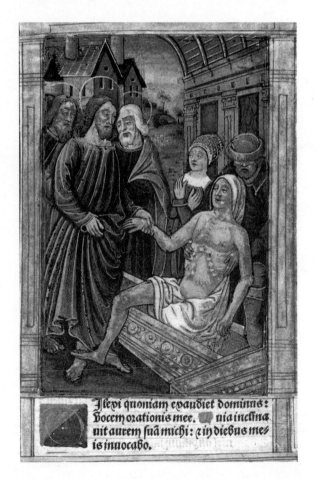

Experiments with Galvanism
Giovanni Aldini, 1804

Italian physicist Giovanni Aldini (1762–1834) famously
applied electric currents to George Foster's corpse after the
murderer was hanged at London's Newgate prison. During
this precursor to modern defibrillation, Foster's arms
and legs reportedly moved and his body began to quiver.
His muscles were "horribly contorted, and one eye was
actually opened".

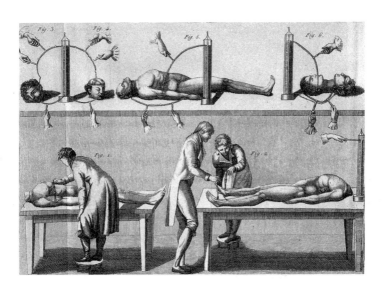

'Designer Dying'
Timothy Leary, 1997

American advocate of psychedelic drugs Timothy Leary
(1920–1996) documented his own death in *Design for Dying*.
This excerpt from the introduction explores consciousness
and the possibility of designing your own 'de-animation'.

Personally, I've been looking forward to dying all my life.
Dying is the most fascinating experience in life. You've got
to approach dying the way you live your life – with curiosity,
hope, experimentation, and with the help of your friends.

I have set out to design my own death, or de-animation as I
prefer to call it. It's a hip, chic thing to do. It's the most elegant
thing you can do. Even if you've lived your life like a complete
slob, you can die with terrific style. I call it 'Designer Dying,'
and it involves two basic principles by which I've lived my life:
think for yourself and question authority.

Related to the many problems one faces in maintaining
a life characterised by self-reliance and personal growth and
anticipating an educational and self-fulfilling death are five
challenging questions:

1 Where is personal consciousness located?
 Answer: One's personal consciousness is stored in the
 nervous system. The brain is the hardware – the bio-
 computer that fabricates and navigates the realities we
 inhabit. The software systems that operate the brain
 are a combination of your genetic makeup and your
 experience – these programs, directories, files, and
 personal operating systems define the individual soul.

2 What happens to personal consciousness when bodily
 functions cease?

Answer: Unless scientific methods of preservation and/or reanimation are employed, when the body dies the brain rots. Your personal software systems crash. Your hard drive is destroyed. If you choose to ignore the preservation/reanimation options, there are two ways to deal with your defunct software: you can be passively buried in a coffin and let it rot in the landfills we call cemeteries, or you can be cremated.

Cremation is more dignified than rotting. Cremation is a choice made by the owner/manager of the brain and is approved by the polytheistic–pagan–humanist religions that glorify the individual's gods-within and encourage reincarnation or reanimation planning. The aim of monotheistic-totalitarian religions is to prohibit individuals from exercising any navigational control of conception, reproduction, and post-mortem transition. Totalitarian religions prohibit cremation.

Although I'm aware of and excited about the emerging scientific methods for reanimation, I have made the fateful decision to forego those options. I will be cremated, and a portion of my ashes will be placed aboard a rocket ship and blasted off into outer space, where they will orbit the earth before disintegrating upon reentry into the atmosphere. I have always considered myself an astronaut, and in death this will become a reality.

3 How can the hardware of the brain be preserved for reanimation after physical death?

Answer: There are three scientific methods for preserving the brain:

      1 Cloning a new brain and body from cells
      2 Cryonic suspension of the body and/or brain
      3 Biological brain banking – awaiting donor transplant to a new body

I recognise that preserving the brain does not assure that the software directories, the memory files and the personal operating systems, will be preserved. Therefore, the owner of the brain must make arrangements to 'save' and 'back up' the memory software that comprises the individual's personality and consciousness of self.

4   How can personal memories and genetic algorithms stored in the brain be backed up and stored for uploading into the new or reanimated brain?
    Answer: Owners who wish to preserve and reanimate their neuro-memories (souls) must diligently collect and protect material mementos that will help reconstruct the unique personality and personal environment of their lives – within reason, of course. The tombs of the pharaohs are fantastic models of personal-reality storage, but impractical for our times. Material items, mementos, souvenirs, clothes, books, and pictures are obviously vulnerable to loss. Remember the tomb robbers.

    The key to software backup, therefore, is digitisation. IF YOU WANT TO IMMORTALISE YOUR CONSCIOUSNESS, RECORD AND DIGITISE.

5   Success in preserving one's personal hardware (body brain) and autographic software depends on supportive environments and stable, highly motivated caretaking organisations. What are the political–cultural–social steps required to protect and reanimate hibernating brains?
    Answer: The basic units for survival during life and hibernation are *in-groups* – small teams linked to other small groups. Intergenerational links are also crucial to keep a system going over many decades.

    The following pages will explore these and many other questions and offer a model for designing your own dying.

As this is the single most important thing you will do your entire life, remember these basic guiding principles, which have guided my existence and work:

> Have a sense of humour.
> Conform to the Laws of Levities.
> Think for yourselves.
> Question authority.
> Celebrate chaotics.
> Increasing illumination and understanding is a team sport.
> Whether it's living or dying... always do it with friends!

Mr Spaceship
Philip K Dick, 1953

In an early short story by American author Philip K Dick (1928–1982) a dying professor donates his brain to be used as the central control system for an experimental spaceship. The designers had intended the brain to work "by reflex only".

Toward the middle of August the project neared completion. They stood outside in the hot autumn heat, looking up at the sleek metal sides of the ship.

Gross thumped the metal with his hand. "Well, it won't be long. We can begin the test any time."

"Tell us more about this," an officer in gold braid said. "It's such an unusual concept."

"Is there really a human brain inside the ship?" a dignitary asked, a small man in a rumpled suit. "And the brain is actually alive?"

"Gentlemen, this ship is guided by a living brain instead

of the usual Johnson relay-control system. But the brain is not conscious. It will function by reflex only. The practical difference between it and the Johnson system is this: a human brain is far more intricate than any man-made structure, and its ability to adapt itself to a situation, to respond to danger, is far beyond anything that could be artificially built."

Gross paused, cocking his ear. The turbines of the ship were beginning to rumble, shaking the ground under them with a deep vibration. Kramer was standing a short distance away from the others, his arms folded, watching silently. At the sound of the turbines he walked quickly around the ship to the other side. A few workmen were clearing away the last of the waste, the scraps of wiring and scaffolding. They glanced up at him and went on hurriedly with their work. Kramer mounted the ramp and entered the control cabin of the ship. Winter was sitting at the controls with a Pilot from Space-transport.

"How's it look?" Kramer asked.

"All right." Winter got up. "He tells me that it would be best to take off manually. The robot controls – " Winter hesitated. "I mean, the built-in controls, can take over later on in space."

"That's right," the Pilot said. "It's customary with the Johnson system, and so in this case we should –"

"Can you tell anything yet?" Kramer asked.

"No," the Pilot said slowly. "I don't think so. I've been going over everything. It seems to be in good order. There's only one thing I wanted to ask you about." He put his hand on the control board. "There are some changes here I don't understand."

"Changes?"

"Alterations from the original design. I wonder what the purpose is."

Kramer took a set of the plans from his coat. "Let me look." He turned the pages over. The Pilot watched carefully over his shoulder.

"The changes aren't indicated on your copy," the Pilot said. "I wonder –" He stopped. Commander Gross had entered the control cabin.

"Gross, who authorised alterations?" Kramer said. "Some of the wiring has been changed."

"Why, your old friend." Gross signalled to the field tower through the window.

"My old friend?"

"The Professor. He took quite an active interest." Gross turned to the Pilot. "Let's get going. We have to take this out past gravity for the test they tell me. Well, perhaps it's for the best. Are you ready?"

"Sure." The Pilot sat down and moved some of the controls around. "Anytime."

"Go ahead, then," Gross said.

"The Professor –" Kramer began, but at that moment there was a tremendous roar and the ship leaped under him. He grasped one of the wall holds and hung on as best he could. The cabin was filling with a steady throbbing, the raging of the jet turbines underneath them.

The ship leaped. Kramer closed his eyes and held his breath. They were moving out into space, gaining speed each moment.

"Well, what do you think?" Winter said nervously. "Is it time yet?"

"A little longer," Kramer said. He was sitting on the floor of the cabin, down by the control wiring. He had removed the metal covering-plate, exposing the complicated maze of relay wiring. He was studying it, comparing it to the wiring diagrams.

"What's the matter?" Gross said.

"These changes. I can't figure out what they're for. The only pattern I can make out is that for some reason –"

"Let me look," the Pilot said. He squatted down beside

Kramer. "You were saying?"

"See this lead here? Originally it was switch controlled. It closed and opened automatically, according to temperature change. Now it's wired so that the central control system operates it. The same with the others. A lot of this was still mechanical, worked by pressure, temperature, stress. Now it's under the central master."

"The brain?" Gross said. "You mean it's been altered so that the brain manipulates it?"

Kramer nodded. "Maybe Professor Thomas felt that no mechanical relays could be trusted. Maybe he thought that things would be happening too fast. But some of these could close in a split second. The brake rockets could go on as quickly as –"

"Hey," Winter said from the control seat. "We're getting near the moon stations. What'll I do?"

They looked out the port. The corroded surface of the moon gleamed up at them, a corrupt and sickening sight. They were moving swiftly toward it.

"I'll take it," the Pilot said. He eased Winter out of the way and strapped himself in place. The ship began to move away from the moon as he manipulated the controls. Down below them they could see the observation stations dotting the surface, and the tiny squares that were the openings of the underground factories and hangars. A red blinker winked up at them and the Pilot's fingers moved on the board in answer.

"We're past the moon," the Pilot said, after a time. The moon had fallen behind them; the ship was heading into outer space. "Well, we can go ahead with it."

Kramer did not answer.

"Mr Kramer, we can go ahead any time."

Kramer started. "Sorry. I was thinking. All right, thanks." He frowned, deep in thought.

"What is it?" Gross asked.

"The wiring changes. Did you understand the reason for them when you gave the okay to the workmen?"

Gross flushed. "You know I know nothing about technical material. I'm in Security."

"Then you should have consulted me."

"What does it matter?" Gross grinned wryly. "We're going to have to start putting our faith in the old man sooner or later."

The Pilot stepped back from the board. His face was pale and set. "Well, it's done," he said. "That's it."

"What's done?" Kramer said.

"We're on automatic. The brain. I turned the board over to it – to him, I mean. The Old Man." The Pilot lit a cigarette and puffed nervously. "Let's keep our fingers crossed."

The ship was coasting evenly, in the hands of its invisible pilot. Far down inside the ship, carefully armoured and protected, a soft human brain lay in a tank of liquid, a thousand minute electric charges playing over its surface. As the charges rose they were picked up and amplified, fed into relay systems, advanced, carried on through the entire ship –

Gross wiped his forehead nervously. "So *he* is running it, now. I hope he knows what he's doing."

Kramer nodded enigmatically. "I think he does."

"What do you mean?"

"Nothing." Kramer walked to the port. "I see we're still moving in a straight line." He picked up the microphone. "We can instruct the brain orally, through this." He blew against the microphone experimentally.

"Go on," Winter said.

"Bring the ship around half-right," Kramer said. "Decrease speed."

They waited. Time passed. Gross looked at Kramer. "No change. Nothing."

"Wait."

Slowly, the ship was beginning to turn. The turbines missed, reducing their steady beat. The ship was taking up its new course, adjusting itself. Nearby some space debris rushed past, incinerating in the blasts of the turbine jets.

"So far so good," Gross said.

They began to breathe more easily. The invisible pilot had taken control smoothly, calmly. The ship was in good hands. Kramer spoke a few more words into the microphone, and they swung again. Now they were moving back the way they had come, toward the moon.

"Let's see what he does when we enter the moon's pull," Kramer said. "He was a good mathematician, the old man. He could handle any kind of problem."

The ship veered, turning away from the moon. The great eaten-away globe fell behind them.

Gross breathed a sigh of relief. "That's that."

"One more thing." Kramer picked up the microphone. "Return to the moon and land the ship at the first space field," he said into it.

"Good Lord," Winter murmured. "Why are you –"

"Be quiet." Kramer stood, listening. The turbines gasped and roared as the ship swung full around, gaining speed. They were moving back, back toward the moon again. The ship dipped down, heading toward the great globe below.

"We're going a little fast," the Pilot said. "I don't see how he can put down at this velocity."

The port filled up, as the globe swelled rapidly. The Pilot hurried toward the board, reaching for the controls. All at once the ship jerked. The nose lifted and the ship shot out into space, away from the moon, turning at an oblique angle. The men were thrown to the floor by the sudden change in course. They got to their feet again, speechless, staring at each other.

The Pilot gazed down at the board. "It wasn't me! I didn't

touch a thing. I didn't even get to it."

The ship was gaining speed each moment. Kramer hesitated. "Maybe you better switch it back to manual."

The Pilot closed the switch. He took hold of the steering controls and moved them experimentally. "Nothing." He turned around. "Nothing. It doesn't respond."

No one spoke.

"You can see what has happened," Kramer said calmly. "The old man won't let go of it, now that he has it. I was afraid of this when I saw the wiring changes. Everything in this ship is centrally controlled, even the cooling system, the hatches, the garbage release. We're helpless."

Sources and Credits

Abu'l-Fazl. The Akbarnāma. Vol. III. Translated by H Beveridge. Calcutta: Asiatic Society of Bengal; 1910. First produced in Persian in the 1590s.

Aldini G. Experiments with galvanism. In J Aldini. Essai Théorique et Expérimental sur le Galvanisme, avec une Série d'Expériences Faites en Présence des Commissaires de l'Institut National de France... 1804. Reproduced with permission of the Wellcome Library, London.

Anonymous. Extracts from a lost (and found) memorandum book. Blackwood's Edinburgh Magazine 1821;8(48):609–11.

Anstey F. Vice Versâ, or, a Lesson to Fathers. London: Smith, Elder & Co.; 1882.

Austen J. Mansfield Park. Vol II. London: T Egerton; 1814.

Belden LW. An Account of Jane C Rider, the Springfield Somnambulist. Springfield: G and C Merriam; 1834.

Bernheim H. Suggestive Therapeutics: A treatise on the nature and uses of hypnotism. Translated by CA Herter. New York: G P Putnam's Sons; 1889.

Bickersteth EH. Yesterday, To-day, and For Ever: A poem, in twelve books. London: Rivingtons; 1866.

Bierce A. An Occurrence at Owl Creek Bridge. In A Bierce. Tales of Soldiers and Civilians. New York: Lovell, Corvell & Company; 1891. Originally published in the San Francisco Examiner, 1890.

Blair R. The Grave: A poem. London: M Fenner; 1743.

Boston Daily Mail. The trial of Albert J Tirrell, charged with the murder of Mrs Maria A Bickford: Before the Supreme Court in Boston. Boston Daily Mail 1846.

Brocas. Stripes of Conscience. In T Grady. No. III, or, the Nosegay: Being the third letter of the country post-bag, from the man to the monster. Dublin: Thomas Grady; 1816. Reproduced with permission of the Wellcome Library, London.

Burnside J. The Dumb House. London: Jonathan Cape; 1997. Reprinted by permission of The Random House Group Limited.

Cheyne G. The English Malady: Or, a treatise of nervous diseases of all kinds. London: G Strahan and J Leake; 1733.

Coleman G. Meditations on Living, Dying and Loss: Ancient knowledge for a modern world. From the first complete translation of The Tibetan Book of the Dead. Translated by G Dorje. Edited by G Coleman with T Jinpa. London: Penguin Books; 2008. Reproduced with permission of The Orient

Foundation. First published in 2005.

Coleridge ST. Letter to Robert Southey. In EH Coleridge (ed.). Letters of Samuel Taylor Coleridge. Vol. I. Boston: Houghton, Mifflin & Co.; 1895.

Collins W. The Moonstone: A romance. Vol. II. London: Tinsley Brothers; 1868.

Conan Doyle A. The disappearance of Lady Frances Carfax. The Strand Magazine 1911; 8(252):815–26.

Cooper RT. The Effects of Chloroform. c.1912. Reproduced with permission of the Wellcome Library, London.

Courbet G. The Clairvoyant or, The Sleepwalker. Oil on canvas. c.1865. Musee des Beaux-Arts et d'Archeologie, Besancon, France / Bridgeman Images.

Crick F. Notes on Consciousness. Manuscript. Wellcome Library 1988. wellcomelibrary.org/player/b18179356 [accessed 4 November 2015].

Darwin E. The Poetical Works of Erasmus Darwin. Vol. II. London: J Johnson; 1806. First published 1789.

Davies O. The nightmare experience, sleep paralysis, and witchcraft accusations. Folklore 2003;114:181–203. © The Folklore Society, reprinted by permission of Taylor & Francis Ltd, tandfonline.com.

Day, FH. Hypnos. c.1896. © Royal Photographic Society / National Media Museum / Science & Society Picture Library.

De Mirjian Studios. The Buddha Pose. In M Agniel. The Art of the Body. London: Batsford; 1931. Image reproduced with permission of the Wellcome Library, London and De Mirjian Studios.

Denslow WW. The Tin Woodman and the Scarecrow. In LF Baum. The Wonderful Wizard of Oz: With pictures by W W Denslow. Chicago: Geo M Hill Co.; 1900. Sourced from the Rare Books and Special Collections Division of the Library of Congress, Washington, DC.

Descartes R. The Passions of the Soul. In R Descartes. The Philosophical Works of Descartes: Rendered into English by E S Haldane and G R T Ross in two volumes. Vol. I. Cambridge: Cambridge University Press; 1911. Originally published in 1649 as *Les Passions de l'Âme*.

Dick, PK. Mr Spaceship. Imagination: Stories of science and fantasy 1953 January. © Philip K Dick, 1953. Used by permission of The Wylie Agency (UK) Ltd.

Dickens C. Oliver Twist. Vol. III. London: Richard Bentley; 1838.

Dickinson E. The Poems of Emily Dickinson. Edited by MD Bianchi and AL Hampson. Boston: Little, Brown, and Co.; 1930. Originally thought to be written around 1863.

Dostoyevsky F. The Dream of a Ridiculous Man. In F Dostoyevsky. Short Stories. New York: Books, Inc.; 1900. First published in 1877 as *Son Smeshnogo Cheloveka*.

Eliot G. The Lifted Veil. Oxford: Oxford University Press; 1921. First published 1859.

Elliotson J. Human Physiology. London: Longman, Rees, Orme, Brown, Green & Longman; 1835.

Fludd R. Tomus Secundus... de Supernaturali, Naturali, Praeternaturali et Contranaturali Microcosmi Historia, in Tractatus Tres Distributa. 1619. Reproduced with permission of the Wellcome Library, London.

Freud S. Psychopathology of Everyday Life. Translated by AA Brill. New York: The Macmillan Company; 1914. Originally published in 1901 as *Zur Psychopathologie des Alltagslebens*. Reproduced with permission of the estate of A A Brill.

Galton F. Inquiries into Human Faculty and Its Development. London: Macmillan and Co.; 1883.

Gesner J quoted in Benton AL. Johann A P Gesner on aphasia. Medical History 1965; 9(1):54–60. Reprinted with permission of Cambridge University Press.

Gold HL. The Man with English. In F Pohl (ed.). Star Science Fiction Stories (No.1). London: T V Boardman & Co.; 1954. Reproduced with kind permission of E L Gold.

Golgi C. Opera Omnia. Vol. II: Istologia normale. Milan: Ulrico Hoepli; 1903.

Graves R. A Child's Nightmare. In R Graves. Complete Poems in One Volume. Manchester: Carcanet Press; 2000. Originally published in *Fairies and Fusiliers*, 1917.

Graves RJ. Observations on the nature and treatment of various diseases. Dublin Quarterly Journal of Medical Science 1851:11(1):1–20.

Gray K et al. More dead than dead: perceptions of persons in the persistent vegetative state. Cognition 2011;121:275–80. Reprinted with permission of Elsevier.

Grice S. Feather Brain. 2012. Reproduced with permission of Sarah Grice and Wellcome Images.

Harris D. Humanoid Robot. 2002. Reproduced with permission of
Dianne Harris and Wellcome Images.

Head H. Aphasia and Kindred Disorders of Speech. Vol. II.
Cambridge: Cambridge University Press; 1926.

Hervey de Saint-Denys M. Les Rêves et les Moyens de les Diriger:
Observations pratiques. Paris: Amyot; 1867. Reproduced with
permission of Yale University, Harvey Cushing/John Hay
Whitney Medical Library.

Highfield R. The mind readers. Mosaic 2014; 20 April.
mosaicscience.com/story/mind-readers [accessed 30 September
2015]. Licensed under CC-BY 4.0.

Hodgson J. What does your inner voice sound like? Writers' Inner
Voices 2015 13 May. writersinnervoices.com/2015/05/13/what-does-
your-inner-voice-sound-like [accessed 24 August 2015]. Writers
Inner Voices is part of the Hearing the Voice project at the Centre
for Medical Humanities at Durham University.

Hoffman ETW. The Sandman. In J Oxenford and CA Feiling
(trans.). Tales from the German, Comprising Specimens from
the Most Celebrated Authors. London: Chapman and Hall; 1844.
Originally published in *Die Nachtstücke*, 1817.

Holloway T. Nightmare. In E Darwin. The Poetical Works of
Erasmus Darwin. Vol. II. London: J Johnson; 1806. Reproduced
with permission of the Wellcome Library, London.

Hopwood AR. False Memory Archive: Erased UFOs. 2012–14.
Photo by Steve Tanner. Courtesy of the artist and The Exchange
Gallery in Penzance.

Hudgins A. Playing Dead. Poetry 2005 July. Reproduced with
permission of Andrew Hudgins.

James W. The Principles of Psychology. Vol. I. New York: Henry
Holt and Company; 1890.

Kafka F. A Report to an Academy. Translated by I Johnston.
British Columbia: Vancouver Island University; 2015. Originally
published in 1917 as *Ein Bericht für eine Akademie* in *Der Jude*.
Reprinted with permission of Ian Johnston, Vancouver Island
University.

Kandinsky W. The Art of Spiritual Harmony, Translated with
an Introduction by M T H Sadler. Boston: Houghton Mifflin
Company; 1914. Originally published in 1910 as *Über das Geistige
in der Kunst*.

Kipling R. The Mark of the Beast. In R Kipling. Life's Handicap:

Being stories of mine own people. London: Macmillan and Co.; 1891. Originally published in the *Pioneer*, 1890.

Leary T, Sirius RU. Design for Dying. New York: HarperCollins; 1997. Reprinted by permission of HarperCollins Publishers Ltd. © Timothy Leary, 1997.

Loftus E. How reliable is your memory? TEDGlobal 2013. ted.com/talks/Elizabeth_loftus_the_fiction_of_memory [accessed 24 August 2015].

Lovecraft HP. Hypnos: A story of weird adventures. Weird Tales 1924; May/June/July:33–35. Originally published in *National Amateur*, 1923.

Luria AR. The Mind of a Mnemonist: A little book about a vast memory. Translated by L Solotaroff. Cambridge MA: Harvard University Press; 1968. © 1968 by Michael Cole.

Macnish R. The Philosophy of Sleep. Glasgow: W R M'Phun; 1830.

Martineau H. Letters on Mesmerism. London: Edward Moxon; 1845.

Marvell A. A Dialogue between the Soul and Body. In GA Aitken (ed.). The Poems of Andrew Marvell, Sometime Member of Parliament for Hull. London: Lawrence & Bullen; 1898. First published 1681.

Maupassant G de. Afloat. London: George Routledge and Sons; 1889. Originally published as 'Sur l'eau' in *Les Lettres et les Arts*, 1888.

Maxwell JC. Recollections of Dreamland. In L Campbell and W Garnett. The Life of James Clerk Maxwell: With a selection from his correspondence and occasional writings and a sketch of his contributions to science. London: Macmillan; 1882. The poem was originally written in 1856.

Melville H. Moby-Dick, or, the Whale. New York: Harper & Brothers; 1851.

Multi-Society Task Force on PVS. Medical aspects of the persistent vegetative state. N Engl J Med 1994;330(21):1499–1508.

Murakami H. Sleep. In H Murakami. The Elephant Vanishes. Translated by A Birnbaum and J Rubin. London: Vintage; 1994. Originally published in the *New Yorker*, 1992. Reproduced with permission of Curtis Brown Group Ltd, London. © Haruki Murakami, 1989.

Nagel T. What is it like to be a bat? Philosophical Review 1974;83(4):435–50. Thanks to the publisher of the *Philosophical*

Review, Duke University Press, and Thomas Nagel.

Pandit JJ, Cook TM. Accidental Awareness during General Anaesthesia in the United Kingdom and Ireland: Report and findings of the 5th National Audit Project. London: The Royal College of Anaesthetists and the Association of Anaesthetists of Great Britain and Ireland; 2014. Reproduced with permission of The Royal College of Anaesthetists.

Parfit D. Reasons and Persons. Oxford: Oxford University Press; 1984. Reprinted with permission of Oxford University Press.

Pinero AW. In Chancery: An original fantastic comedy in three acts. New York: Samuel French; 1905. First staged in Edinburgh, 1884.

Poe EA. The Premature Burial. In EA Poe. The Works of Edgar Allan Poe. Vol. VI. New York: Funk & Wagnalls Company; 1904. Originally published in the *Philadelphia Dollar Newspaper*, 1844.

Prince MH. The Dissociation of a Personality: A biographical study in abnormal psychology. New York: Longmans, Green and Co.; 1906.

Proust M. Remembrance of Things Past Vol. 1: Swann's Way. Part one. Translated by C K Scott Montcrieff. London: Chatto & Windus; 1951. Originally published as *Du Côté de Chez Swann*, 1913.

Ramón y Cajal, S. Human Neonatal Astrocytes. c.1904. Reproduced courtesy of Cajal Legacy, Instituto Cajal (CSIC), Madrid.

Robertson R. The Halving. In R Robertson. Hill of Doors. London: Picador; 2013. © Robin Robertson. Reproduced by permission of the author c/o Rogers, Coleridge & White Ltd., 20 Powis Mews, London W11 1JN.

Schiavonetti L. The Soul Hovering over the Body Reluctantly Parting with Life. In R Blair. The Grave: A poem. London: Ackermann; 1813. First published 1808. Reproduced with permission of The Trustees of the British Museum.

Seabrook WB. The Magic Island. London: George G Harrap & Co. Ltd; 1929.

Shakespeare W. Romeo and Juliet. In W Shakespeare. The Plays of Shakespeare in Nine Volumes. Vol. IX. London: William Pickering; 1825. First published 1597.

Shelley MW. Frankenstein, or the Modern Prometheus. London: Lackington, Hughes, Harding, Mavor & Jones; 1818.

Sherrington C. Man on His Nature: The Gifford Lectures, Edinburgh 1937–8. Cambridge: Cambridge University Press; 1942. Reprinted by courtesy of the University of Liverpool Library.

Sherwood. K. Golgi's Door. Mixed media on canvas, 20 x 20 inches. 2007. From the collection of the US National Academy of Sciences.

Stevenson RL. The Strange Case of Dr Jekyll and Mr Hyde. In RL Stevenson. The Merry Men and Other Tales and Fables. New York: Charles Scribner's Sons; 1895. First published 1886.

Thoreau HD. The Writings of Henry David Thoreau, edited by Bradford Torrey: Journal, vol. II. Boston: Houghton Mifflin; 1906. The diary entry is dated 12 May 1851.

Turing, AM. Computing machinery and intelligence. Mind 1950;49:433–60. Reprinted with permission of Oxford University Press.

Unknown artist. 'Animal Magnetism'. 1815. Reproduced with permission of the Wellcome Library, London.

Unknown artist. Count Karnice-Karnicki's Invention. In W Tebb et al. Premature Burial and How It May Be Prevented. 2nd edn. London: Swan Sonnenschein & Co.; 1905. Reproduced with permission of the Wellcome Library, London.

Unknown artist. Fudō Myō-ō. 17th century. Reproduced with permission of The Trustees of the British Museum.

Unknown artist. Raising Lazarus from the Tomb. 1510. Reproduced with permission of the Wellcome Library, London.

Unknown artist. Sarah Bernhardt Asleep in Her Coffin. c.1882. Reproduced with permission of Stanley B Burns, MD and The Burns Archive.

Unknown artist. 'The Dream'. 1970s. Reproduced with permission of the Wellcome Library, London.

Unknown artist. 'The Dream'. 1970s. Reproduced with permission of the Wellcome Library, London.

Unknown artist. The Effects of Liquid Chloroform. 1840s. Reproduced with permission of the Wellcome Library, London.

Van Eeden F. The Bride of Dreams. Translated by M van Auw. New York: Mitchell Kennerley; 1913.

Wells HG. The Stolen Body. The Strand Magazine 1898; 16(95):567–76. Reproduced with permission of United Agents LLP on behalf of The Literary Executors of the Estate of H G Wells.

Wiertz AJ. L'Inhumation Précipitée. 1854. Reproduced with permission of the Wellcome Library, London.

Zola É. Thérèse Raquin: A novel. Translated by E Vizetelly. London: Grant Richards; 1902. Originally serialised in French in *L'Artiste*, 1867.

Author and Artist Index

Index